WAXING
Pathetic

Copyright © 2019 M. B. Clark

TABLE OF CONTENTS

INTRODUCTION:

What? You wanted poetry? Oh, I have that stuff tattooed right here. I figured it was the only way anyone would actually read it.

Waxing pathetic. Waxing poetic. Waxing philosophic. Waxing politic. Waxing lunatic. Just a lot of waxing...of the literary kind, not the spa kind. I don't go there. I can shave myself. The last thing I need is another stranger focusing on yet another area of insecurity.

It is just the nature of my chaotic life and these times that drives me to capture the essence of both. The quintessence. The umbrella theme of *pathetic* seems to cover the majority of this material. And my pathos does matter. Striving for mass appeal is a fool's errand, after all. I can only hope that I can somehow connect with a few readers who are a bit more adventurous than the average Jane or Joe who have both been chomping on fairly formulaic fodder over the years, so much so that their literary teeth are rotting. We will drill down and fill these cavernous cavities with solid divergence.

In regard to the last book, the impetus to write it was basically: *Why be greedy with my own tragedies? I should spread out the burden, give it all away. Social media will suck me dry anyway.* Yes, that last book was pansy ass. This one will have a backbone...and guts. It will cut even closer to the bone, suck out all the marrow, and regurgitate it. In this way, I will capture more precisely the actual conundrum of the inner workings of my so-called brain, as it also attempts to slice and dice through American society at large, like a ninja. So yes, there is some stream of *un*consciousness involved. More like a River of Hades. But for the reader's benefit, I do use the traffic signs known as punctuation marks. This is my marked improvement on that James Joyce kid.

Pathetic. I like the word. It's not sad...it's more like pitiful. It kind of wallows around and whines a lot, even though the whining is probably justified. It also connotes a certain obsessive cyclical pattern. A pathetic pattern. A train of thought that just keeps picking up where the caboose left off. I, for one, would prefer to leave my caboose at home most of the time. Unfortunately, it's just always there, taking up space, pulling up the rear, and not very well.

How and why does a person become pathetic? Where does it start? I won't say that I have been pathetic *all* my life, but certain episodes and entire phases of my life definitely fall into that category. Some of the most pathetic material I have is in my high school journal that I scribbled on during class and when sitting on top of the dryer in the basement at night to avoid my family and stay warm. I did not spend precious moments of my adolescence writing about my tribulations for nothing. And since I am an immature and sentimental type, I still have all of this material at my fingertips. Is that pathetic too? I'm 50-something. Well, I for one am damn proud of my immature heritage.

Anyway, I am sure there are plenty of people out there who want to walk down my memory lane with me, as pathetic as that is. Most of the journal entries included here are in the original voice of the teenage girl that I was at one time, but I had to step in as, you know, the adult, kind of a Ghost of Merry Future, at certain points, to have a chat with her. But don't worry, this book contains much more than just these blasts from the past. It will also include the deconstruction of said blasts, and the continued line of development from my stellar personal history to my present-day worldview that lacks a Harvardesque pedigree, yet is steeped in bold experience gleaned from coddled college towns, the mean streets of Small Town America, the asphalt insane asylum of Los Angeles, and the star-dusted streets of Las Vegas.

This book has five parts:

Part 1: Been Down This Road

This is the section where I dredge up the most mortifying scenes from my youth and then attempt to connect the personal to the professional to the political, as in *why is this happening to me? Oh yeah, I'm a liberal. Again, it was those commie parents of mine, so concerned about social and environmental justice. Ugh.*

Part 2: This Is How I Do It

This part blithely addresses the unbearable lightness of the undoing of mid-life. Some of it reads like a comedy routine, because that is what mid-life is.

Part 3: Pushing the Envelope

This is the part where I accost the reader with further meandering, horrifying anecdotes of loss and heartbreak, albeit embedded in an undertone of *this is not my life*. New word—Meanderthal: Meandering Through It All. There are some tales of cancer in here but feel free to skip over those parts if

A. You are sure cancer will never happen to you.

B. You don't wish to be reminded of this mortal threat.

C. You believe that no self-respecting author should punish a reader in this manner.

Part 4: This Is Real...and Surreal

You will just have to read this part with the understanding that the author is now dog-paddling through her underdeveloped political intellect, confronting her eroding self-image, and grieving the loss of the idea that was America. Might just be treading water at this point.

Part 5: Bouncing Back Again

Jumpstarting a life after multiple near deaths. Is it possible? This is about resilience. And of course, still sexism with a side of ageism.

Yes, this book is a work of fiction. There are no references, and my recollection and regurgitation of anything and everything is certainly to be taken with a shaker of salt. But if the reader chooses to believe that I am recalling events as they actually occurred, that is his or her choice. It is "a novel" because as soon as anything hits the page, unless it can be cross-checked and verified by a number of independent entities, and since the author is by definition both fallible and highly suspect, it must be fiction. This is material that is based on the most absurd parts of my life, which I have probably misremembered, misunderestimated (Bushism), and then tweaked here and there for effect. Fiction. Definitely. Not only is this fiction, it is possible that all of American culture is fiction too. Your net worth could even be fiction.

On the other hand, this work may not even fit any category or genre, so maybe it is "A Novel...Approach." Of course, I had to investigate the theory that the conventional plot structure (foreplay, climax, resolution) originated from the structure of the male orgasm. Female orgasms are much more complex and nuanced, from what I hear. Thus, "women's" literature should reflect that fact. This book does, anyway. So if you are a man, consider it a semi-guided tour of one woman's trek towards multiple variable intellectual orgasms.

I should add that perhaps I was drawn to the underground (yes, this book does go there) partly because I wanted to go undercover, like Gloria Steinem did at the Playboy club. It took guts, (and a degree of desperation) because there is the chafing between being a "respectable" upstanding member of society, and working in *that* world. There is still a stigma in certain circles. Stormy Daniels is not everyone's patron saint, and I can't understand that. She has become a lightning rod in the women's movement. I suppose I am biased.

Anyway, I wanted to know what it was like to do that work. I wanted to discover what I could learn about society, men, sex, women, and human nature. Perhaps, due to this fact, this piece of literature is not so much a meta-memoir, but *feminist literature*. Whatever you wish to call it, that will have to be fine with me. Ultimately, any writing I do is based on the radical notion that a woman's (even this woman's) voice, experience, and thoughts *matter*. To what degree and to whom, is also something beyond my control. It's a perennial political question: *Who really matters?*

So when I am not staring off into space, pretending to write, making organic macaroni and cheese for my mother who doesn't know she's a mother, working out to 80s rock, or lying on my yoga mat gazing up at the glass ceiling (or in my case, the debt ceiling), I am coming up with a scheme for world domination—or enlightenment, as the case may be. Trust me, it's gonna be big. Yuge!

Some people complain that my transitions are abrupt, and I jump from one episode, time frame, or topic to another, but I am merely subverting expectations and avoiding predictability, to ensure the reader that no algorithm wrote this stuff. So come on, keep up with the ADD, and let's go for a wild ride!

PART I
Been Down This Road

Is this what my life has come to? I am an experienced live entertainer. *No. I perform ridiculous lap dances in dirty clubs. At the age of 52.* Hey, I still look amazing. This is a triumph. *No. It's a tragedy. My knee is looking more and more like my mother's knee.* I brought my head back up to check on the guy. His eyes were closed, he was slack-jawed like a trout, and his ugly Hawaiian shirt hung open (since I had unbuttoned it). At least he didn't have a huge gut, just a little pooch. Bald, but not terrible looking. His cologne stuck to my skin and in my nose. I felt the kink in my neck. How did I wind up here in this dark, foreboding place, dancing naked for people who did not care about me in the least? Why was this man on this couch letting a strange woman try to turn him on? From the feel of things under my ass, I was having an effect. My choreography involved a variety of inverted positions since inversion is supposed to make you age backwards. So no, I was not performing a BJ (I know that crossed your dirty mind), just my normal yoga routine.

My iPhone timer had just passed 7 minutes. Still 8 more minutes to go. *Make conversation.* I glanced at the picture of the Eiffel Tower.

"So have you been to Paris?"

He opened his eyes. "Uh, no. You have?"

"Yeah, when I thought I was dying, I felt the need to check a few things off the ol' bucket list, you know."

"Dying?"

I was sprawled face up across his lap at that point, taking notes on the ceiling.

"Yeah, a few years ago. Cancer, you know. They ripped everything out. See my scar?"

I sat up to straddle him and drew his attention to my midsection that had become the prime target of all sorts of renovation plans and a major source of insecurity. I sucked it in and sat up ramrod straight.

"Oh, that doesn't look too bad," he lied.

"Well, thanks for saying that. I guess my boobs still upstage that problem area." I giggled and reversed myself on his lap, leaned back to one side and brought one leg up behind his ear.

"So…do you have any kids?" I asked.

The timer alarm went off after he had gone on about his kids and the DJ had played Aerosmith. The host knocked on the door and rolled it open and patted his wrist to indicate the time was up. I rolled off

Baldy. "Would you like to go for another round, sir?" the host asked. They rarely do.

"No, I think I'm good."

The host skittered away.

"Ok, well, come back and see me sometime." I gave him a quick hug, and he was off.

I gathered my bra, hitched myself back into it, pulled my sweaty socks back on, and zipped up my knee-high boots. Sigh. *Ok, only need a couple more of these today and I can get the fuck out. Need a new bed. Bed. Bed. Bed. $3000 with the adjustable base. I'm worth it.*

So how did it all begin? What possible chain of events led to this sweet, educated, organically raised girl being in a strip club doing VIPs and showing off scars with whomever wants to spend his spa money? I mean, I was smart enough. (For what?) I went to college, a good one even. (So what?) But I majored in dance at a time in my life when that was (and still is) all I really wanted to do (and writing stuff like this too). And is dancing while naked the only way a dancer can make consistent income from dancing? I believe it's true. Is that right? Does it matter?

Back when I had made this horrendous decision and announced that I intended to move to the big city, my daddy told me, "You better marry a rich man or you're going to wind up a prostitute." Prostitute? Now how does that work? That sounded scary at the time. I mean, I sort of understood what prostitute meant, but I did not understand what marriage meant. I had not yet figured out that marrying for money is essentially prostitution. I should have asked for a bit more clarification.

Let's go back in time. To the very beginning.

In 1975, I was in love with my third-grade teacher. He had dark hair and professor-type (hipster) glasses like my dad did, and even though he sounded like Kermit the frog, he was my idol. My desk was the closest to his desk, and I was always "working ahead" and making up writing assignments for myself and handing them in whenever I felt like it. I was the coolest third grader in that tiny two-bit school of 300 kids.

June 1975, 10 years old, letter to my teacher:

I wish I could do magic and fly and that stuff. I watch TV shows like Bewitched, and she flies around all the time. It would sure be fun to do that. I would fly around all day. And I could see Lee Majors! That would be fun. I could twinkle my nose and have my desk up in the air too and when I want to hand in a paper I could make it fly down into the "inbox." Well, I think you get the picture.

I am bewitched to this day and look how prophetic I was about the flying inbox. It's email.

September 1977, 12 years old, self-assignment:

My Five Wishes

#1 I wish to meet Shawn Cassidy. Not because that's what everyone would wish, just to meet a star, but because he is the only person I am the least bit interested in. I like him because he's intelligent, has a great personality,

he's a good singer, and he really seems to be my kind of person. We have so much in common.

#2 To achieve my goal in life, which is to get into show business. I want to be a singer, a dancer, a songwriter, and a guitarist. And I am not planning this just because that's what Shawn is doing. He's not a dancer, and he's not really a guitarist. I have loved to sing and dance since before I started school.

#3 I'd like to be a person everyone would like. I think if I were a little less shy, I could be. I like to make other people happy. I like to give instead of get.

#4 I am very interested in stopping pollution, and saving our natural wilderness and endangered species. I am also looking forward to the day when solar energy will be used all over the country. I am going to start a club that's going to do something about this.

#5 To WIN against Tracy Jackson on Field Day!! I can't wait to see her face! Boy, will she be mad! I also hope to get a ribbon in some other event too.

I'd also like to do something really heroic, like stand up for someone else's rights. I wish I could have worked for equal rights for women and Black people. I think it was terrible the way they didn't have equal rights.

Note my clever tactic of using one wish to achieve a whole set of goals and adding an addendum of heroism.

So. Meet a star, be a star, be an activist, and be an athlete. Did I meet these goals or not? I have met stars, but I am not a star (yet). The other goals are pretty accessible since they are unpaid positions. My

12-year-old self is tapping her toe waiting for the star part to commence, and she isn't convinced that I have been all that heroic in any tangible way. Still plenty of opportunity to work for equal rights. She's a bitch of a boss, that 12-year-old me. Yet note how the first goal is about a celebrity and most of the other goals involve becoming a celebrity or being heroic. Both of these are the result of too much exposure to popular culture and media, but also due to my deep-set opposition against being an "ordinary American." That term is so insulting to all Americans. Once in a great while, one might hear about "everyday heroes" or "unsung heroes." These are just bones the media throws to those who do have to work for a living in the middle or lower classes. But by and large, the media worships those who are just fabulously wealthy, regardless of how they got that way.

December 1979, 14 years old.

Well, the dance was last night. Would you believe it? I didn't dance with anyone! Not one guy! I was ready for a bad night, but not that bad. But if that's the way it is, then that's the way it is. And that was my last dance.

I don't like life anymore. I guess Mom is right. My shyness is killing me, just getting in the way of everything. I don't think anyone in this whole world really loves me. My parents have to; I'm their daughter. Well, Mom might love me, but I don't believe my dad does at all. He's constantly moaning, "Where did I go wrong?" and "How did you get so weird?" Not very understanding. I've got to clean out that barn for my horse. I want someone else to talk to and confide in, someone who will always listen.

So then I started my political career, since I needed someone to listen to me. (That's a joke.) So in sixth grade, circa 1980, I decided to enter a speech contest with the topic, "If I Were President." I honestly thought I had all the answers and would make a fine President at the time. This was my winning speech. I remember it because it was a nerve-racking experience at 14 to speak in front of people. And to have a need to be the best. I have to remember all the times when I did win in life. It helps. Keep in mind, this was during the presidency of that sweater-clad peanut farmer, Carter, who went on to greater things after his term.

IF I WERE PRESIDENT

If I were elected President in 1984, I would be the first female President in American history and it would be about time. It would be like a breath of fresh air to have a woman in office instead of another hard-nosed executive-type man. But things would probably be a lot more difficult for me than they would be for a man. The public, especially men, would be a lot more critical of me than they would be of a man. It would be quite a difficult task to prove to everyone that I was capable of doing a good job. But women are not to be considered the weaker sex any longer. We have more than proven that we are equal to men, something that never should have needed proving in the first place.

There are many areas that I would work on if I became President. First of all, I would do my best to keep the nation out of war. Second, there are some very good reasons why we should not boycott the Olympics. Third, there is a lot of important work to be done developing new energy sources. And finally, I believe the American people need improvement.

Now of course if we're going to have a woman for president, then like-wise there should be women soldiers going to war. There are already a lot of female volunteers in our military, and our Armed Forces are now so dependent on women that they would find it difficult to go to war without them. Even if the plan to register women for the draft does not go through, women are destined to see combat in any future war involving the US. But if I were President, I would try to see to it that we stay out of war in the first place. Why must nations quarrel with each other over everything? Wouldn't it be better if there were no nations, no boundaries, no divisions of the earth? It's too bad the world isn't that way. It would prevent a lot of problems if we could all just get along as one world. Pulling out of the Olympics is an example of this. We don't like how Russia is playing, so we aren't going to play on their playground. The Olympics should never be influenced by politics. It should simply stand for peaceful competition among the best amateur athletes in the world. If we boycott the Olympics, we are depriving our athletes of their dream of Olympic medals they have been working towards for years. The world would work better if we thought of ourselves as citizens of the world, not just of our own country.

We could get along on about half the energy we are using now. By using less energy, people might actually become more creative and constructive since there would be less TV, pinball machines, discos, amusement parks, and driving. We use more energy for entertainment than for the bare essentials.

If we cut back on our energy usage, I believe we could supply all our energy needs with the sun and wind. These are two natural, renewable, clean sources of energy that can last forever. Doesn't this make more sense than to squeeze every last drop of oil and ounce of coal out of the ground? We thought it would last forever, so we put off the development of renewable non-polluting sources. There is an end to oil and gas, but no end to the need for energy.

The National Academy of Sciences recently released a report on what our energy priorities are until the year 2000. Some of the statements made in the report bothered me. It said that although nuclear power has its risks, it's cheaper and safer to use than coal. Now to me, that just can't be right, because if there was a mining accident, then some miners might get killed. But if a nuclear accident occurred, thousands of people might die on the spot and many others later on, from cancer and birth defects. The land, the plants, and the animals would also die, plus the air, water, and land would be contaminated for many years. We might never be able to live on that land again. Even the hazards of mining and burning coal aren't half as bad as that.

The report goes on to say that solar energy is too expensive to supply more than 5% of our energy needs until the year 2000, but according to my research, solar energy now supplies more than 6% of our energy and that's twice as much as nuclear power. The director of the Solar Energy Research Institute says we can surpass 20% with solar power by the year 2000, and that solar cells will be an economically competitive option within a few years.

So if I were President, I would slowly stop the nation from importing oil. I would demand more development and more encouragement of solar power and wind energy. Conservation is an absolute must and will be forever. Switching to solar energy would do a tremendous favor for future generations.

Rosalynn Carter once said this nation's greatest resource is its people, and she's right, but unfortunately it seems to me that the quality of the majority of people is going down. The only way to improve this nation is to improve its people, and the place to begin is in the schools. The

education system in America is not at its best, and it seems to me educa-
tion should be rated as the most important issue all the time. Teachers
and students ought to have friendly relationships in order for the students
to get a better education. Teachers have to care about the kids, help them
as much as possible, and give more of themselves to their jobs. After all,
they are influencing the adults of tomorrow.

I don't believe enough people in America work hard enough to achieve
their goals, if they even have any. They are not that optimistic these
days. There is no enthusiasm for the future. Kids should not wait until
their junior year in high school to begin to think about what they want
to do. Goals should be a permanent fact of life at every age, even if the
goals change every month. We used to be a very great country, but not
so much anymore. As a country, we have many goals to work towards,
but everyone must help. We can't expect the government to pull things
together for us. We are all part of the problem unless we work together
to make this nation greater than it ever has been before.

Jesus. I sounded like a young Republican. Well, at least in the dig for
smaller government and making America great again. Sad that we still
haven't met the goals for solar and are still addicted to oil.

Then came high school and the inevitable devolution of the mind due
to the influence of **hormones**. Drugs are a bitch.

Oct 20, 1980

I think I've done or not done a terrible terrible thing. There was a party
at Jim's house on Saturday, and Kevin was there. From what Rhonda just
told me, I think he was wishing I was there.

Forget that! I'm so fucking mad at Kevin I could strangle him. He got stoned out of his skull at that party, which was on the night before my birthday. He forgot about my birthday probably because he was too drunk to remember today and just innocently asked me why I wasn't at the party. I said I thought I didn't know Jim that well. I hadn't been invited. Later, I called Rhonda and she filled me in on a few things that happened. It was a lot of drinking, of course. She didn't drink much, but Kevin did. I hope his liver shrivels up, the asshole. Some people tell me he's going to ask me to go with him sometime, but I don't know whether or not I would accept or even believe his sincerity. I hope he's satisfied; he's wrecked my life.

Now we'll go on to Tommy. He's just another son of a bitch, and I'd love to tell him off! He's only using me, lying to me, toying with my heart. Why can't guys just be honest? Can't they just tell me how they feel instead of acting like they've forgotten me? Because I know they haven't.

I may be wrong about all this. They both may care very deeply about me. But I don't know. After last weekend, I just don't know. Even if I asked them both, do you think I would get the truth? Kevin's birthday is this Friday, and I intend to get him a card. Then maybe he'll remember that he forgot mine. But he probably won't. Motherfucker. I wish I'd never gotten involved with either of them. They've caused me nothing but heartache.

Then I quoted some lyrics from the disco song "Upside Down" by Diana Ross. Music was always my go-to for dealing with disappointment. I think it is this journal entry in which I began rendering invectives against men. And it had to be my dad who taught me these words.

Oct 25, 1980

Tommy will be here in 20 minutes!! Yipes! I'm scared to death! I have never even been out on a date, let alone with a fantastic fox like Tommy Johnson. If my friends could see me now—they wouldn't believe who I was going out with! Never. This is like me going out with Troy or Barry or Steve at my old school. Unheard of! They would be so jealous of me because Tommy is even better than all of them, much better. He even sounds cute on the phone, even though he also sounds far away.

Now it's 15 minutes! We're going to a movie, probably at University Park, then "get somethin' to eat." That's what he said. I wish I was more experienced in dating, then I wouldn't be so scared, but to get experienced you've got to start, so I've got to go through this. Really, I wouldn't miss it for anything.

There were pig testicles on the cutting board. My dad was slicing them up and putting them in a pan on the stovetop.

"Oh, these are a delicacy. You won't even know what you're eating."

Tommy was going to arrive in the next fifteen minutes. The porker testicles gave off an aroma that was a cross between french fries and burnt liver. There was no way in hell I was going anywhere near that.

"You know Tommy will be here in fifteen minutes and I am not ready yet," I yelled as I raced upstairs. "Could you please at least move that off the counter?"

My hair felt smooth as I wrapped it around the barrel of the hot curling iron. I wanted to look like Farrah Fawcett for my first date. The iron *almost burnt the edge of my ear, and my wrist ached as I held it in the awkward position that would give my hair the flipped-back style I had to have. I stared at my face in the mirror. Am I pretty? I curled my eyelashes and used mascara for the second time ever (that pink tube of Maybelline with the curled brush). The smell of the pig nuts was wafting up the stairs, and I tried not to inhale through my nose as I finalized my outfit and added pink heart earrings. I was feeling very trendy since I had just had my ears pierced at the mall.*

Meanwhile, Tommy had come to the door and my mom had let him in. He had spilled gasoline on his hands on the way over and asked to use the sink to wash. When I came downstairs, Tommy was washing his hands next to pig nuts, my mother was looking at me like it might be the last time she ever saw me, and my dad was still slicing and dicing the pigs nuts. But I looked good! I had picked the perfect bell bottom jeans and a soft pink sweater with a cowl neck. Tommy turned around and saw me after drying his hands, and his green eyes glinted as a huge grin spread across his face.

I jumped off the stairs and hustled towards the door, and he met me there. "Okay, bye," I said over my perfect coiffure. "See you later. Not sure what time it will be." And we ran out into the crisp October air, with just hint of manure smell in it.

In the car, I mentioned that I couldn't believe it was snowing already and that I had to run in it.

"How far?"

"Eleven miles."

"What? You are too dedicated. That's crazy."

"I just don't want to slough off and get out of shape. It's too hard to try to get it back."

He went on and on about track and how he ran any event our coach wanted him to. He was a really good pole vaulter. Once he fell backwards on top of the coach and they fell off the pit and onto a bolt that left a huge bruise on the coach's leg. He told me stories about everything that happened last track season, since I was a freshman and had been at my old junior high school last year.

"You know, everyone in both towns knows we are going out."

"Really?" I was shocked. Tommy was so popular that everyone in the whole county knew his social plans. He was a fantastic athlete, especially in wrestling. He mentioned all the people I knew who were popular in my old school: Tim, Barry, Mike, Dave, all of the guys that I had crushes on when I was there.

"Your parents seem worried about you."

"Yeah, I guess." I wasn't going to say it was my first date.

We got there a half hour before the movie started, so we wandered around the mall and met some of his friends. We stopped at Burger Chef to get something to drink.

"I still can't believe I am out with you," I mumbled, with my eyes cast down.

"So shy," he said.

"I talk a lot when I'm not nervous. It's just that I wasn't popular last year. But being out with you makes me feel like now I am, sort of."

"I can't believe you weren't popular."

"Well, you don't know what I was like last year. I still had braces. When I started school here, I didn't expect this."

He continued to ramble on about all the great things he'd done in wrestling.

As soon as we settled in near the wall in the movie theater, he announced: "Hey, here come my parents." *I snapped my head to look at him, and he laughed.*

Then came the good part. He took my hand and held it on my leg. He rubbed my finger with his thumb, very gently. Something inside me melted. We clasped our fingers.

He leaned over and whispered, "Is this your first date?"

I glanced down and mumbled, "Yeah. No reason to lie."

He left once and came back quickly, then we just put our elbows on the armrest, but soon he took my hand again and said, "I liked it better when I was holding your hand." *We kept shifting arm positions trying to get comfortable, until Tommy finally took my arm and put his under and around it. So his arm was on the armrest underneath my arm and my elbow was on his side of the armrest. Our hands were clasped on the armrest. Get the picture?*

It was freezing outside after the movie. He teased me about remembering where the car was. He put his arm through mine and chattered his teeth. We ran a little ways to the car. It was even colder in the car and he turned on the heater. While waiting for it to warm up, he put his arm around me, leaned over, and I turned my head to face him. I couldn't see his face, but—then he kissed me! It happened so fast and all I thought was kiss him, stupid! So I did. It was sweet. I loved it. But it still felt awkward. I don't know. I wish I could've seen what we looked like, then I'd know.

We went to his house—just so I could see it, and then he drove me home. I thought he might kiss me again. I hesitated before getting out.

"Thanks," I murmured.

"I'll see you Monday," he replied.

Something else escaped my lips but I can't recall what it was, something dumb I suppose. He didn't drive out till I was in the house.

Ok, maybe that was not that pathetic, but actually somewhat poignant. Depends on who's reading, I guess. How many girls in 1980 wrote down a play-by-play of their first date, right down to the position of the hands during hand-holding? Some might call these small details quite meaningless and tedious, but there is more than just the devil in details. Quite often life and death are embedded in them. No one can make a movie of any impact without sweating every detail. Just watch *Dumb and Dumber*. Or any of those Bourne movies. In this case, I spent the rest of my life trying to recapture that little spark.

On Oct. 28, 1980, Tommy gave me a note, along with his picture. This was major. He wrote it in pencil, so I traced the letters in ink, for posterity's sake. His main point was that he thought I was "too nice," and he did not want to ruin me. The next day, I was counseling myself. My parents could not afford a shrink.

Oct. 29, 1980

Tommy is a nice guy, but he's not what I am looking for in a person. He's cute with a great body, but his mind is not at the level I'm looking for. He doesn't get good grades. He's stuck-up. No. He's not the type of guy I'm searching for. That person may not even exist. He has to care about people, the world, the environment, and me. He has to be thoughtful, intelligent, and similar to me in more than a few ways. We should have relatively similar views on life and love. He's got to be in good shape, athletic in some way, sweet, affectionate, mentally strong, ambitious, optimistic, creative, modest, honest…like me! I could never be with a guy who had no opinions, and he has to actually be able to defend the ones he does have. Like I said, this person does not exist. But I will fall in love anyway, because I know I will overlook all the negative qualities.

Sunday Nov. 9th, 1980

Very happy now! Just got back from Tommy's house. We went canoeing down the creek behind his house. I'll never forget this. It was a beautiful day today. The sky was a deep bright blue, and it was a little windy. I had never paddled a canoe before, so we ran into the edges and got stuck a few times, but it was fun.

"Are you going to take driver's training this summer?" he asked.

"I don't know."

"Don't."

He laughed. He had his hands on my shoulders, and then he bent down and kissed my neck and whispered in my ear.

"You're beautiful." He kissed my neck again and said, "Gimme a kiss."

So I did.

I was in love.

We watched some football in his den, then played a game of Othello and I beat him. At 6 pm, my dad called, and I told him I'd be home in an hour. We were sitting on the floor, leaning against the couch. Somehow a pillow fight ensued, and he kissed me in the aftermath.

When we got in the car to take me home, that was when the Big Kiss happened. It seemed like forever until he let me go! He put his arm around me on the way home, so I had to work the stick shift, with him directing.

"You're just like a little child," he said softly, partly to himself.

Then he leaned over and said, "You're learning." And kissed me again.

When we got to my house, he kissed me again before I got out.

So let me count the kisses...

The first one in the car on our first date.

The second one was last Friday after he brought me home from the game.

The third one was in the canoe.

The fourth one was in the den.

The fifth, sixth, and seventh were in the car on the way home or after we got there.

The third and the fifth were the very best! Should I keep track of this or should I lose track? Seven kisses already, five in one day! I wonder when the next one will be and what it will be like.

My friend Lori told me that he was probably the best kisser in the school. I guess she would know, being the gossip-monger she is. I know first-hand how good he is now. He is probably the best guy in the whole school. How lucky am I? I've seen him three weekends in a row.

Let's unpack this pathetic discourse, shall we? I can't navigate a canoe, a stick shift, or a kiss, but I know football, and beat him at board games and pillow fights. Apparently, I understood the competitive things, not yet realizing that kissing is also a competitive sport. I learned a lot that day, including how to count kisses. And my dad called. He was worried about his little girl getting taken advantage of by the captain of the football team. Pretty sure they did not like him at all. But they didn't like any guy who was ever with me, like most parents.

Nov. 11, 1980

He wouldn't have let me sign his yearbook if he didn't really like me and plan on liking me for quite a while, right? There were only autographs from girls in his yearbook, no boys, and there weren't very many autographs. Plus they were all long entries, so I think he only let girls who really mean something to him sign it. And now that I signed it, it's kind of like I have established myself in his life as a girl he'll never forget and someone he really cares for, I hope.

Yes. Guys don't sign other guys' yearbooks. That's gay, and they can't write anyway. But this entry is so pathetic it hurts. It is an omen of dark days ahead, days wasted pining away for some worthless person of the opposite sex. Ugh.

Two days later, I followed up with:

I guess I shouldn't worry, but I sure do miss him. I've got to see him this weekend or I'll die. The memory of Sunday is fading, but it still makes me feel good to think about it. Seven kisses! Seven times to heaven! Two of them sent me flying—the one in the canoe, and the one in the car before we left his house. He said, "Hey, come here." And he put his arm around me and we leaned over to each other and that kiss felt like it would never end. I never kissed a guy like that before. It has changed my whole life. I miss him so much that I feel like looking for him after class.

Hormones. Out. Of. Control.

Dec 19, 1980

These days are getting hard to believe. Yesterday was the jazz lab concert. Tommy was in the audience, and I broke out in a cold sweat as soon as I saw him. Tammy told me afterwards that he had been staring at me the whole time! And today he wrote me another note! Deb delivered it for him. Can you believe that? He actually wrote me a note! When the note found my hand, I looked at it like it was a mirage. What would it say? Is he mad at me again? Then I ripped it open and read the first few lines and almost fainted.

Last night at the game, he actually talked to me! I was headed for the concession stand, and he was coming towards it on my left. I have the feeling this rendezvous was not a coincidence. He walked up to the stand just as I did and sidled over towards me. He greeted me first.

"Hi."

"Hi." I smiled and glanced away.

"Did you read the note?"

"Yeah."

"You looked kind of unhappy up on the stands. You were shaking your head and stuff."

I smiled and shook my head. He had been watching me. I had felt it.

"I noticed you haven't been putting in as much mileage lately, only about 130 miles last month."

"Well, you can't run hard all year."

Then his friends came around, and that was the end of that.

Later on, he was standing at the bottom of the bleachers and I caught his eye as I looked down at him and he looked up and winked at me. It was the sexiest wink I had ever seen! I felt that old feeling again, that mix of fear and excitement and sparks popping out of my gut. He looked over at me while we were on the bleachers. We were on the same level but far apart. His friend Steve came over and talked to me and Michelle, who had come to the game with me. We talked about sports and gossiped about other runners in track. Michelle said Kim had been doing drugs, and this was shocking to me. Was that how she was edging me out? I vowed to blow her cover and get rid of her. I couldn't wait for the next year because she would be gone and I would rule supreme after training all summer. I would work on fast stuff, race distance, and about three long runs per week, 50 miles per week, 200 per month.

So Tommy had finally come to his senses. He seemed to at least want to be friends again, but the wink indicated more. Was he still scared? If so, how long would he be scared?

Dec 21st 1980

A lot happier now. Yesterday I ran 11 miles to make sure I could still do it. Considering the hills and winter weather, 1:40 isn't such a bad time. I skied over to my favorite road, switched shoes and ran, and then came back to my skis which I buried in the snow. I almost froze to death on the way back home. Since then I have been dreaming of Tommy. I know I should not be getting this way about him again...but I can't help it! There was something in that wink. The note, the wink, the smile, the few words...it must all mean...well, I'm just not sure. Not at all. Seeing me onstage must have done something to him, as I'm sure he wrote that note right after the concert. Tammy told me he had been staring at me the whole time, and I definitely felt someone's eyes on me. I could hardly control my fingers on the strings. He had written that people do crazy things when they're scared. Then he wrote that he was scared. Is he saying he did a crazy thing by dropping me? Does that mean he's not scared anymore? Those little things he did makes me think he isn't. Maybe I'm all wrong. He just wanted to apologize, explain himself, and nothing more. I'll try calling him tomorrow. I still have a lot of shopping to do before Christmas.

Last night I did get hold of Tammy. I read her the note, and she said it was sweet. I told her I didn't know what he meant when he said I could look right through somebody. She said it was hard to explain what he meant, but that I did have a way of doing that and it was a good thing, that I make people feel different. Tammy has a way of making me feel much better sometimes. I'm going to get stuck-up if I don't watch out! No, I don't think I will. I'm too shy, too afraid to talk to strangers.

Yeah, he loves me. He might flirt with others, but that's just because he doesn't know if he can really have me. I think we will get back together, sooner than I think. I want him back more than anything. He needs me! I need him! We were so right together. This past month could have been one of the best months of my life, but instead I had to try to live without him. I haven't been sad, just angry and resentful. But now it's all love when I think of him. I know I am supposed to be too young to love someone, or even to know what love is, but damn it, I think I know when I love someone. Believe it or not! Parents. They sure know how to be wet blankets. They cannot quell the fire of adolescence.

Okay, fine. I added that last line last month. That fire burned out of control for a number of years. But I didn't start it. Not my fault. Hormones are forces of nature. These forces forced me to hang all my hopes on one man or another for years. Only natural. And there was of course the unnatural social pressure to get married and procreate. I know there are solo women out there. And maybe they are happy. But maybe they could be happier. We all just make up our minds to be happy even when there are just as many reasons to be unhappy. Perspectives shift. I find that I can think more clearly without all those hormones racing around. But I miss the racing. Sometimes.

Dec 22, 1980

2 days till Christmas. I'm not that excited about it. The only thing that excites me is Tommy. I decided not to call him. "Play it cool," dad says. Something tells me I should not write a note. But what does he want? I keep reading his note over and over, searching for clues. He didn't write Love, Tommy at the end. I'm probably going hyper over it for nothing.

March 1981

After crying and falling apart behind the school, I had been walking back into the school and he came running out to his car with someone else. I can't handle him right now. I turned my head toward the school and said "No!" out loud, but I don't think he heard me.

"Hey, you," he called as he raced by.

I turned my head as he was nearing his car, not me.

"Hi."

"You going to the dance?"

"I don't know. Maybe."

"I want to talk to you later on if you're here."

"Sure."

He hopped in his car and drove off.

My stomach lurched. I steadied myself. And I inched my way back to the building. Tammy was there in the hallway.

"Alan was really hurt because you left. He really likes you, you know. He's always talking about you."

I had been outside between the game and the dance for over 45 minutes, so I guess everyone thought I left. I looked into the loud noisy flashing room, and the butterflies flew. I heard a good song being played and decided to be crazy enough to go in. I paid, got my hand stamped, and was just standing there, and the principal asked, "You want me to keep your change for you?" I fumbled. He laughed. "No, no, I don't want to keep it for you."

I walked towards the lights like a zombie deer in the headlights. Tammy and Denise were trying to get me inside as I was baby-stepping my way in, but then out of nowhere Tommy loomed in front of me. He blinded me. Just bam. And I ran back out the door.

I threw my purse down on the sidewalk and ran behind the disco productions van. I saw the principal come out of the school, so I ducked down. I was so afraid of him finding me. He would never understand anything. Maybe I really was crazy. I was just a person having a nervous breakdown, that's all. If I hadn't run off, everyone would've seen me break down into tears, including Tommy, and that would've been the worst. I would've had a heart attack.

Like a masochist, I pulled myself together enough to go back in. Tammy was there again. She helped get me in the door. Finally, I loosened up and danced with Alan, Kevin, and Bobby.

I had been sitting next to Alan, and then I watched Tommy walk out of the dance. I knew he wasn't leaving, but I had an urge to follow him. But before I did anything that stupid, he came back in. I wanted to go up to him and ask him if he still wanted to talk to me. But I just stood there swaying in limbo, glancing back to where Tammy was, and keeping one eye on Tommy. He looked over to where I had been sitting, and then he saw me standing there like an idiot. Him and a friend of his came over to me and he asked, "You dancin' with somebody?"

"No."

He started to take me onto the floor, as his friend teased us. "May I have this dance?"

"No, no, she likes me better."

We walked side-by-side with arms around each other out to the floor. When we started dancing (it was a slow dance, of course), the first thing he asked me was:

"What's the matter?"

These words uttered from this exact person sounded like the most beautiful music I had ever heard.

"You."

"Me? Why is it me?"

I finally blurted out, "I miss you. I can't help it."

"Okay, calm down. It's okay." He rubbed my back. We were so close. It felt so good; the cure for my frazzled nerves.

"Why don't you call me?" he asked.

"I didn't think you wanted me to."

I touched his hair.

"I always wanted to touch your hair."

He smiled and asked why.

"I just wanted to."

"Why didn't you before?"

"I never got a chance."

He held me tighter.

I zoned out the rest of the time.

At the end of the dance, before he left, he came over to me, took my finger, and said, "See you Monday."

"Yeah."

We looked at each other as he turned to go. He didn't smell like pot. He was not high. I knew that for sure. I can tell.

The next time I went running, I stopped at Tammy's house and she was walking out to see me. She told me Tommy and I looked beautiful and *that he looked like he did care. It sure felt like it. I could literally feel the love flowing through his body into mine. You know there's a good possibility that he didn't get high because of me and what happened at the last dance. I have seen at least part of what is underneath that facade he puts up.*

March 31, 1981

Well, I guess if you want to make headlines, taking a shot at the President is a surefire way. The world is in terrible shape, and no one is doing a damn thing about it. I think of all the people in this crummy school not even wanting to help keep the world from falling apart. Depressing. People here make a joke out of the suffering in the world and they make fun of people who are trying to do good. They are only feeding their body and not their soul. What's the point of feeding a body if the soul in it is starving?

I'm so sick of school. I want freedom. Can't I just leave? I think I will tonight, after my speed workout. It'll be Goodbye little town blues, I'm catching the first train for the coast. It will be a fantastic adventure! That's what I need. Even if I got kidnapped or something, who cares? It would still be an adventure. A better idea might be to just go hide out in the wilderness; just walk away from the school and find a hiding place and just stay there, getting food any way I can. Like a raccoon or a lone wolf. No one would see me. No one would find me. I'd just disappear. Do I have the guts to pull off a stunt like that? I'll think about it while running. Maybe today could be my last day of school, with no more first days. I suppose I would be risking a whole lot of consequences if I did it, but I'm smart enough to avoid them.

If only I could just live my life and stop trying to find answers to questions that can't be answered. Damn it, I cause myself so many problems that way. I make life harder than it has to be. But there's no way I can stop the questioning. Is my life going to make a sad story? Or will it have a happy ending? Maybe it will be a comedy.

June 15, 1981

Oh happy day! I saw him today. I think I have a dual personality. I read something about that in a psych book somewhere. Maybe I'm reincarnated. I keep having that deja vu feeling. I should always write after I run when my head is clearer. Sometimes the things that seem insane at first really make a lot of sense when you give them a little more oxygen.

When we were at Molly's the other day, he immediately started checking out her lawnmower. (You thought I was going to say some body part, didn't you?) So now I know that he is mechanically inclined. He could find a lot to fix at my place.

Today:

Up at 6:30

shower dress breakfast

biked to school at 8:45

Films, talk, test

Mark!

Biked home at 1 pm with traffic, heat, and hills

helped fix tractor

herded a few cows

laundry

wrote article

ran 7 miles with hills

talked to myself about Mark

shower

made supper

And then I would watch some bullshit 80s TV show like *Flamingo Road*. Talk about being Wonder Woman. And to this day I still think I'm an underachiever. I guess because there was never any pay off for all the overworking I did in high school and college. And speaking of fantasies, how about *The Love Boat, Dallas, Dynasty*, and of course *Fantasy Island*? De plane. De plane. Could it be that my expectations both of life and of men were heavily influenced by the escapist TV of the 80s? And what about the impact of films like *Flashdance, Working Girl*, and above all, *Pretty Woman*? What a feeling. In all of this, the man plays an essential role in the success or happiness of the woman. How does a girl ignore these subliminal messages?

(Back to 1981)

Just one of my normal days. Should have left out the TV and Mark. I caught sight of him outside right before I opened the door to leave the school building. I could have caught myself, but I didn't. I was fuming about my report card. I got an F on my final exam in Algebra! It stuck out like a sore thumb. But my final grade was a C– so not catastrophic for the GPA. Okay, where was I? Oh, yes. Well, I was upset so I showed him my report card so he would understand why. I should have gone out the other door and just pedaled past him. Wish I had the will.

I wish I could just dance for a living. I'd never be depressed if I could just dance all my troubles away. Music never fails to cheer me up, unless it's sad music. It can affect me more than the weather. On rainy days, I can be incredibly happy with the right music. But sad music on a sunny day can pierce my heart. Sometimes the sky is just so beautiful it makes me cry because I know it is fleeting. Dance is actually the art form that is most like life because it is the most ephemeral.

June 17, 1981

I live in this notebook. In my pages. With my pen. At least I can rely on them. Never depend on people. They're all out to get me. Everybody's out to hurt me, embarrass me, tease me, use me. Can't they see things from my point of view? Can't they try to put themselves in my position? But why would they? They have to care enough first. They'll never know how it feels. I'm too young to feel so old. Too young to think like this, to have to go through all this. It seems like I get out of one critical phase and I'm thrown right back into another crisis. One of my old teachers always asked, "What's fair in this world?" when I complained. Nothing. Nothing whatsoever is fair. I work and work and work and wait and wait and wait, but nothing comes of it. Meanwhile, there are others who don't deserve anything, but they get more than me, and more than a lot of other people who might be more deserving than I am. Deserve. What does that mean anyway? To deserve something? Who is to judge who deserves something? The weather isn't fair. Fate has no sense of fairness. Time isn't fair. A person cannot go through life assuming that if they just work hard enough, then it's only fair that they'll get what they deserve. Hard work is no guarantee of anything except blood, sweat, and tears. These are bitter pills to swallow for everyone. No sugar coating here.

If something is "meant" to happen, does that mean I don't have to do anything to make it happen?

I don't know what to do about Mark. If I could just talk to him, everything would be fine. He can always cheer me up. There are so many forces pulling me in so many different directions.

I anticipate something from him when I shouldn't. I should never expect anything from anybody. But like anybody else, I just want a little attention and respect.

I have to run 15 miles today, and I can't let this stuff stand in my way. If I think the wrong things while I'm running, I'll break down in the middle of the road and never make it home. Mountains of meaningless words. If only I could find the words to say to him. Should I let him read my journal? When I was near him today, I just stood there, too shy to say anything. I was sure something was wrong. I guess I'm just too emotional and too serious for people, but I won't change to please them. I won't. But I don't even understand myself, so how do I expect to understand anyone else? And how can I expect anyone to understand me? Sometimes I just want to give up. I just need somebody I can count on. He has a good outlook on life. He's never down for long; he recovers quickly. That's why I could tell something was wrong today. Maybe he was just tired.

June 18, 1981

Planting in the field. Almost all day. Now the thing is broken again. It should be fixed in time to do more today. Mom and I will probably plant past dark, so that means no running for me today. Well, maybe I need a day off. I did 16 miles yesterday.

I remember picking rocks out of the field where my brother lives. We walked alongside the backhoe like some chain gang tossing stones into the bucket. I rode the back of the planter in the summer to make sure the rows were straight. I did the same on the cultivator to make sure my brother wasn't ripping out rows of soybeans.

"When you have a family business, you have neither a family nor a business." That's what my grandfather said.

It's true.

What a "day off." Trying to stay on that hot, dusty, bumpy planter for hours on end. Can't wait for planting to be done. We can't go on much longer, it's getting close to July. Seems like the days are picking up speed. If I can run 16 miles now, I should be in good shape for that marathon in September. I'll do a few 20 milers in August. Have to maintain some leg speed so I won't have so much to get back after the marathon. I'm way ahead of myself though. Most first-time marathoners do 18 miles twice in the last month before the race.

June 21, 1981

During the last mile of my 14 miles today, the wind kicked up and the rain came and I was drenched in a second, and then the rain blinded me. It was great!

I miss Mark. I know I should be able to be happy just with nature and from within, but I need someone else with skin on to love me. Maybe if I felt more loved by my family, I wouldn't feel so needy. My so-called friends don't seem like friends, just people who think it's fun to terrorize me. Someday my life won't be missing something all the time.

Someday.

I lose one thing, and then try to get it back and I lose something else while in the process of chasing the other thing. But who cares? Why do I write all this? No one cares.

Haven't cried for days and nights.

But I've hurt just the same.

Guess I'm getting a little stronger—

Something good can come from pain.

No one gets it. Mom and Dad are too busy. My brothers, well, I can forget them. They need to grow up some more. They'll start hitting some tough spots in a few years, and maybe they will start to figure out what I'm talking about. But they will never know how it feels to be a girl. I wonder what kind of sister I might have had. I know I'm not the only lonely one. Every woman is lonely for sure. Everybody's got a hungry heart, in the timeless words of Bruce Springsteen. It feels like love is only for those in the middle of everything. Strong, experienced people. Not me. It's like that line from the poem "The Heart of a Woman" by Georgia Johnson: And tries to forget it has dreamed of the stars, while it breaks, breaks, breaks on the sheltering bars…

June 28, 1981

It's a miracle I'm still alive. All I thought about yesterday was pain. For the last three days I just don't know what has happened to me. I think the pain has been building up for about three years now. Hurts to remember any of my life before that. It must be this total lack of any appreciation, respect, or attention. I feel like I'm just a slave to Mom and Dad; they're just bosses who give me room and board. They'll never understand how much some of their words hurt me. They must think my life is fine like I have no problems, no pain, or they just don't think anything because they never even consider my life at all. They think I can handle it all on my own, but they're wrong. I'm their daughter for crying out loud. They think they're so smart, but they're neglecting their own children. All Dad thinks about is farming, his finances, and his anger at various people. I don't think we really know each other in this family. I think he would choose money and land over his family. He treats the dirt on his farm better than he treats us.

I'm physically, emotionally, and mentally drained. I couldn't run today, so I'll have to run 16 miles tomorrow. I've got to pull myself together and try to rise above these awful days, just add them to my stockpile of pain. The only way to melt that ice block of pain is with love. Mark is the only answer. If I ever needed a guy in my life, it's now. But does he need me? Please, God, let him see. Someone has to see. Enough is enough. Enough loneliness already.

I got over Mark by the end of the year. I had to. He started dating my best friend. But someone else was on the horizon as I transitioned away from the drudgery of pure athletics to the cauldron of dramatics and made a new group of friends in the theater. All of the backstage drama upstaged anything that unfolded onstage. We enacted *Annie Get Your Gun, A Midsummer Night's Dream, Whose Life Is It Anyway?* And, of course, *My Fair Lady.* That last title just sends me down the road of comparing all the perennial stories of being rescued by the Prince. *Pretty Woman, Cinderella,* and *My Fair Lady* are the same story line. So are countless other movies. There must be some nugget of truth in there. Is there something wrong with wanting to be rescued? Or even just accepting help? YES! No one should allow themselves to be in need of rescuing. But think of it: Does anyone actually put themselves in need of saving? Isn't it just circumstances? Has society gotten to the point where a single woman can get just as far as a woman with a productive man to help her out? Two wallets, as well as two heads, are better than one, are they not?

I met another boy from one of the plays who I thought was "the one." He was the one for the prom anyway. I was one of the few sophomore girls to get invited to the senior prom. Wow.

May 16, 1982

He picked me up at exactly 6:10. I was wearing this long pink thing with long sleeves that made me feel not one bit trendy or (heaven forbid) sexy in any way, but rather matronly. I almost tripped on the dress coming down the stairs. He watched as I stood there just staring out the window as Mom pinned on the corsage, and then he had to fix it. He had to get it perfect. Mom took three pictures. And he just headed for the door after a quick "Goodbye, nice meeting you." We were already late. And he hated being late.

During dinner we talked quite a bit about how other people see me. We talked about egotism. He thought one should feel proud of themselves. I thought he was a little bit too proud. Maybe I didn't have enough self-esteem. I guess in order to get respect you have to act like you already have it.

I had lost the presidency of my class by one vote. That surprised me. I didn't think I had that much support. Maybe people did respect me. Then he did not speak kindly about the girl who won. That hit me the wrong way. Did she do him wrong in some way? What did he have against her? Was he just trying to make me feel better?

It was early when we arrived. The gang was just trickling in. We sat at a table with his friends. The band was kind of loud, and I was not in the mood for a fast dance nor did I have the guts to go out there and make a fool of myself with him.

We walked around, then rode on the elevator. I think he just wanted to get away for a while so he could kiss me. I felt like I was falling in love. I stopped being afraid of getting hurt. I knew he felt a lot for me, and I became sure that he was not using me. And that even if it ended when he went away to college, it was beautiful and worth all the time and effort. I decided I would get over it.

We got out at midnight. We had Asti Spumante in the car. That was my first experience with the bubbles. It tickled my nose and seemed a little acidic, but it was fun. I knew I could never drink hard stuff like whiskey, vodka, or rum.

Stupid. I wasted so much paper writing about this guy in 1982. He wound up going to law school and forgetting all about my pathetic little insecure self, left behind to endure another two years of mediocre depressing high school.

May 27, 1982

A lot of people make the mistake of judging everyone by the same set of standards: their own. They think that their standards are everyone's standards. Some people have their own individual set of values and standards. *People label certain acts as crazy, but labeling things is insane in itself. Everybody is in a different life situation, and each has his or her own way of dealing with it. The first to do things her own way is considered crazy only by fools. Those who judge others are the ones who are crazy or at least quite ignorant. They're being intentionally insensitive to what it means to be human. I think we're actually entering into an age where humans need lessons in how to be human.*

Dec 16, 1982

I'm sorry I can't seem to live right because I don't know what's right. I'm sorry that I'm sorry. Well, for God's sake, what AM I supposed to do? I don't know how to live. It's a total mystery to me. Everyone else seems to live without all this crap I go through. I hate people who act like they know it all. Maybe they do know a lot, but they don't have to act like it. I defy anyone to figure me out. If I can't do it, it's not possible. I just don't belong...anywhere.

I want to run away from this place. I want to be free, free, FREE! The weight of life is getting unbearable. Every person makes me so sick. I am entirely screwed up. I'm going to start believing people when they say I'm strange. I am. I do need a psychiatrist. I'll never be able to be a teacher or counselor, because I can't even teach or counsel myself. And my writing is just insane babbling to myself because I'm crazy. And this is not okay? I can't stand living with myself! Maybe I am the sick one, not society. I'm not strong. I'm a weakling. I really can't care anymore—about me, about life, about anyone.

I wish I could be kind, but I'm not strong enough or wise enough to be kind when I hurt so much. I just feel so confined, imprisoned...

I think I will quit school!

Jan 5, 1983

Life is NOT too much for Merry Clark! I don't care if I get a D in algebra and a C in chemistry. Who cares?! Why should I base my whole life and self-image on what grades I get? That is so profoundly stupid and self-destructive. Me and chemistry and algebra just don't get along. I'm simply not good at the stuff. Why should I be?

Then, as if I had been squeezed through the eye of a needle and had come out as a budding hippie radical, all my writing started questioning the powers that be. This started when Reagan was elected, and the cold war got fired up. It seems politics was the only thing that could make me stop obsessing about a boy. Unfortunately, politics is still mostly obsessing about a boy.

Oct 31, 1983

My sociology teacher does not believe in the soul. She's just like that. Like everything is rational in her mind. I wish it were that way. Can't think of much that makes any sense in society. Can't anyone be a product of their own making and not wind up being pigeon-holed by a certain culture? Can't we be "manic-depressives" simply because of the fact that our own individual nature is inclined towards emotional extremes? Should such "extremists" be seen as abnormal and be given a label? Why do we have preconceived notions about how any given person should react to any given stimulus?

Some people see no reason to believe in the soul. What does it do? Why is it important? How can one divest the social sciences from the humanities?

How are the humanities really separated from religion? Is nothing sacred then? Why does the school perpetuate intellectual pigeon holes? Why can't I have any voice at all in deciding my own course of study? Why am I at the mercy of a curriculum decreed by a group of adults who don't know me? Why should anyone else determine what anyone else should learn? Am I compelled to listen to anyone? Are we as students ever encouraged to challenge a teacher's choice of method or materials? Would that be dangerous somehow?

Nov 1, 1983

In 4th hour fiction we read Fahrenheit 451 *by Ray Bradbury. We never discussed it. The test on it did not provoke any thoughts about the ideas underlying the story, which some of the class may have missed. Some people don't read. Some people read a book, enjoy it, and then forget it. Others make connections between books and society and their own lives. What accounts for these differences? Explain Emily Dickinson's choice of isolation. She needed to think. Doesn't everyone? Our environment presents various alternatives to each individual, but what accounts for the actual choices we each make is our own free will. Or maybe there is no such thing. Prejudice gets implanted in childhood and grows throughout the school years. Beliefs might as well be treated as fact, because to the believer, they are facts, regardless of any evidence to the contrary. They are reality-proof. We have to have discussions in school, debate that gets to the bare bones of a topic; the philosophical underpinnings. Controversy keeps us alive. There's always too much to say. Always another angle.*

Nov. 29,1983

According to my meager research, it appears there is a fine line between the practice of American democracy and the theory of communism.

What about our prisoners? How much do we really know? How much is hidden behind the iron curtain of government? Are we to judge a person by his or her political views? "The State" is supposed to further the good of all. We need to blend the aspects of capitalism, democracy, socialism, and even maybe communism. When there are violently opposing sides, neither side will ever make the other side compromise.

Who really runs America? The people? Which people? Capitalism appears to breed more greed than socialism ever could. Is the American school system different from a communistic government? Since students have no voice in how the school is run, schools cannot be seen as democratic institutions. Why not try to give students a voice in the institution that most affects them? They might just take an interest in it.

No person is born evil. One can only be made evil. And if a person can be made evil, they can be unmade evil.

June 1984

What kind of world would we have if everyone except valedictorians were wiped off the face of the Earth? Everyone would be fighting over who is the smartest and who should rule. Constant wars. Well, we have that now, so... We each contribute what we have to offer: ourselves. Before I had other creative intellectual people with whom to compare myself, I felt I was closer to life somehow, in all its warmth and pain. I keep telling myself to stop the comparisons, but it's almost compulsive. It's this constant chasing of self-assurance in my own head. Well, yes, he may be smarter, but I am more creative. Or: Yes, she may be thinner, but I am smarter. Or: Yes, he may be richer, but I am not an asshole. It's always apples to oranges because we are all a different type of fruit. Yet we are all fruit. An apple and an orange are both fruits. We are all human. Not sure if the human-fruit analogy really works. Is there a standard "good" human being? I guess a lowest common denominator would include not committing crimes, but lots of people who are believed "good" have probably committed crimes under the radar. Can't I have my own definition of what kind of person is valuable? What is the nature of our value? It isn't like we are just a statistic on some spectrum of good and bad. What is the real utility of measuring people? What is the purpose? Just to label, judge, and classify—and therefore, limit. Categories are limits. Boxes. Prisons.

Humans are a maddening mix of qualities and flaws. Whenever you find out what someone really thinks of you, you're always surprised. Especially after you realize they're right. Then terror sets in. I resent it when others try to pin down my problems on all four corners saying, "There. There's your problem right there." As if they invented it.

Labels like "creative," "different," "special," "talented" have little meaning unless in some context. Was I any of this before someone used these words to describe me? My sociology teacher has some elitist views that I tend to disagree with. I believe that everyone has the potential to be creative and intelligent, but she thinks these traits are mostly genetically endowed. I believe environmental influence and one's own free will account for a lot more success than she believes. Why am I so much more creatively inclined than my brothers are, for example?

On June 21st, 1984, a short opinion piece was published in the local paper.

Graduates Move on to Significant Year

Many people are considering how much of George Orwell's 1984 is reality today. It is probably someone's reality, somewhere in the world. Therefore, it is part of the global consciousness. One man's suffering causes the world to cry.

Just three days before the 40th commemoration of D-Day, when all the world was locked in silence as it listened to the tragic and triumphant D-Day events, the 1984 Cassopolis graduates moved out into the world as hopeful adults. This year is significant in many other ways: the Presidential election, the Olympics, and a record-setting budget deficit. And according to the Chinese calendar, it is also the Year of the Rat.

If one has read 1984, one knows that the rat is a significant creature in the novel. He is portrayed as the symbol of a certain madness, voracity, and deranged power. He is the instiller of the greatest fear and is the most potent persuader. The baccalaureate address at the graduation raised the issue of "moral garbage and academic garbage." Rats love garbage. They make their homes there. While I do not believe that anyone could ever be labeled a rat, no matter how immoral he/she seems to be, I do think there is a rat in each of us. If we are self-aware, we can keep the rat subdued, but the rat can, at any time, gnaw away at one's soul. This is more likely whenever there is increased fear and hate on the loose.

If there is garbage within us, there is probably garbage surrounding us. I am talking about the poisons in our atmosphere and in the water we drink. We are putting man-made poisons into our bodies and souls. How we treat the Earth reflects how we treat each other and ourselves. If we can't change as individuals, then we cannot change the world.

There is much reiteration of the proverbial "real world" at graduation time, as if 12 years of schooling was not real at all, not even connected to the real world. Where have we been for the past 18 years? In some sort of cult fantasy-land? What we mean by this term is competition. We must now compete on a larger stage for resources, mates, respect, love, and security. It's an unprotected "jungle out there." This mentality can scare young people into submission, and it can contribute to the development of a dog-eat-dog attitude. How can these attitudes build a brighter future? They are based on fear, and again, fear runs counter to positive change. The real world lies within, where fear and hope compete for domination on an infinite playing field.

Sometimes we sacrifice our freedom now for what we think will bring us increased freedom later. The reason for this sacrifice is always money. How much of our lives will we spend in the mad chase after the Almighty Dollar? The choice is ours, not the economy's. We do not have to do work we hate for an inanimate object that does not care who has it, in industries or companies that do not care about us. We can work for ourselves and for humanity, realizing that the two are one and the same. This often requires honest self-analysis that most avoid. But our powers of self-awareness remain our only defense against ideological enslavement. We wake up to a new world every day, and we can and must continue to change and grow along with it, while keeping our basic principles as a guide.

Some things never change.

It is often said that the personal is the political. Perhaps part of this book is a pathetic quest to unearth that connection in my own life. My pathos matters!

PART II
This Is How I Do It

(**B**y now, you are probably wondering how I got through my boy-crazy phase, the high school angst, and the bad grades in the STEM subjects. I didn't. I still have all that going on. Somehow, I got into a decent college. I must have written a kick-ass bullshit essay, and they had to meet a rural female quota. Oh, yeah, and they always ask about the education level of your parents. That's really none of their business. But my weakness in the other subjects has been a drag my whole life, so I now have nothing to do but try to write more kick-ass bullshit and hope that some guy needs to meet his rural female quota. Anyway…it's going well.)

Now that I have provided you with a backstage pass to my upscale backstory, complete with a taste of my life as a doe-eyed 15-year-old who was hell-bent on changing Mr. Peaked in High School, I will go ahead and rip on society at large, because I'm good enough, I'm smart enough, and gosh darn it, people like me on Facebook. This is America, after all. I like to circumvent the system, like a good politician does.

Actually, it will be kind of a meandering through the tangles in my head interwoven with yelling at society for causing said tangles. Because let's face it: American society is twisted. So we have to be too. And we don't even know how twisted. We are all slowly boiling frogs. If you are in a pit, you don't really know how high or how thick the walls are. You can go nose-blind to your own shit.

Ok, so maybe I'm a narcissist. A navel gazer? Nobody's perfect. Get over it. Actually, a long time ago somebody told me that nobody's perfect, and I told him to speak for himself. It's a lot of pressure being *so close* to perfect because people look even harder for flaws. Especially in women. So I finally took it down a notch or two because I just started to feel guilty about making everybody else feel so bad about themselves. I realized the reason women point out their flaws—it's to save others the *work* of looking for them. You have to let them know that you know what they *might* figure out about how flawed you actually are. Kind of like running interference and intercepting the darts. You know, masochism, in general.

It turns out that is the best way to be endearing to others: Tell them all the ways you are screwed up. Then they know you are one of them, or even better, *beneath* them. Helping another American feel superior to you is the best way to make them your friend.

"Do you see how you create your own anxiety?" my college counselor once asked me.

Could she see something I couldn't?

If there is one thing I did learn in high school, it was that pretty is not enough. It was never going to be enough for me. I wanted to be super smart, hopefully super pretty (or at least not fat) and never care about how popular I was. I wanted the strength to be free from insecurity of the lowest kind, even if I could not find any reasons to feel secure. But I did not know at the time that this meant I would look like a bitch to everyone else, and when I realized that—you know, when people started to hint that they thought I was a bitch—I thought that maybe being a bitch was a problem. A character flaw. Now I realize that it is absolutely essential to be a bitch. If being a bitch means having self-made standards and expressing your disapproval of bullies and beheadings and the oligarchy and climate change and parabens in shampoo, then bitch on! Just be a bitch who rocks at everything and forces the world to raise its fucking standards. The future depends on it.

So my life has veered between two extremes: "Fuck you! I don't care what you think and I don't need you!" and "*Please* love me. I need you. Please please love me." (Is that borderline personality disorder or bipolar? I get them confused.) It's the higher standards that screw with my personal needs...because a "standard" is just an abstract, not earthbound. It's always something higher in the sky, something that's always just out of reach, since it will automatically move farther away as soon you get anywhere close. But life would be no challenge at all without moving targets, whether we are pushing boulders uphill or chasing a rolling stone or throwing stones at the glass ceiling or just rolling downhill... It's all a ball in play. All fluidity. We hold things in our hand or in our mind just long enough to think we are holding them. And then they are gone. Gone with the wind. Gone in sixty seconds. Gone girl. Gone fishing. You get the idea.

Old movies. Yes, and old TV shows like *Bewitched* and *I Dream of Jeannie*. There was *Wonder Woman* and *The Bionic Woman* and that woman in the perfume commercial who could bring home the bacon, fry it up in a pan, and never never let him forget he's a man. What? So women have been brought up on impossible images of what a woman is *supposed* to be and do. You must be effortlessly gorgeous every minute, twirl around on a dime, look great in a bodysuit, stop bullets with bracelets, cook dinner by blinking your eyes, call the man in the room "Master" because he let you out of your bottle, twinkle your nose to time travel when necessary, cast spells to make your husband look good to the boss, have superhuman strength to catch all the bad guys, and of course rock it in the kitchen, the bedroom, and the work world. And I am out of breath.

Thankfully, I have narrowed my playing field. Well, at least in the area of computer games. I only play *one* computer game. I can proudly say that I have finally *focused* my efforts in this competitive arena, and I have honed my skills to an incredibly high degree. Gotta pick your battles, right? So now I totally rock at match.com. I feed them lies, and they feed me dinner. It's a total win-win. Just like politics. Also saves a lot on groceries. And that makes me smart.

And since we are going down this road...at this moment I am a divorced 53-year-old cancer "survivor" who is still unjustifiably selective. "Cancer survivor." What does this mean anyway? Just means I've had barely enough medical intervention to keep me on the streets causing trouble, or at least lying online, as the case may be. But seriously, is this in any way a *marketable* package? What are my *options* at this particular juncture?

Christianmingle anyone?

Cancermatch.com?

Farmersonly?

Ourtime?

Maybe we should merge match.com with eBay and just get on with the auction.

So on a first date these days, there is no time to waste, so I am straight up honest right out of the gates. Just lay all the credit cards on the table. "Hey, uh, I want you to know that I have cancer, I'm self-unemployed, and I do have some credit card debt. I also have a spot on my cheek right *here*, my neck is getting loose, my thighs need lipo, and my vagina is a little on the dry side. But don't worry, I got this." That almost always leads to a second date, especially that dried-up vagina part. Sets up a challenge. Kind of like when I was younger and I told them,

(Southern accent) "I don't think I've ever had an orgasm, now that I think of it."

(John Wayne) "Well, I'll help you out with that, little lady. You just wait right here while I go get saddled up."

I'm still waiting. Taking him a long-ass time to get saddled up. Slow cowboy.

I just want to find the love of what's *left* of my life…I guess. Since it's obviously too late for the love of my *life*. That ship has sailed. And alas, he was not on it. I really think he missed the boat. And that would be just like him. Or maybe it was the *Titanic* or something. Yes, that's it. I am past the collision with the iceberg, done rearranging deck chairs (I like to work ahead), and the band stopped playing a long time ago, but I still hear music. So I am now just out here in the middle of the

Atlantic, floating on a door, hoping someone rescues me before I fucking freeze to death.

Things are working out.

Meanwhile, the guys are *still* just estimating how many words they have to listen to before they can get sex. How many words exist? He'll never make it. He will never hear enough words from me in order to *earn* sex. So he will wind up stealing sex. At least that's how I see it. What man deserves sex from any woman?

"Til death do us part" used to sound like a fucking *long* time when I was in my twenties. And thirties. And forties. That is a joke, right? That's just flat out insanity. I mean, how do I know where I'm going to be by then? But now...oh, that's like next week, I can *totally* make it now. *I can get there from here.* This is a good time to make that promise because chances are higher that I *will* be able to keep my word.

But have you noticed that now they say, "...as long as you both shall live"? After all, why ruin a beautiful wedding by mentioning *death*? Like it's some sort of life sentence. Or death sentence. Those are pretty much the same thing, after all.

Little story for you:

When I was 12 during the 1970s, I used to talk to my BFF on the only phone that was upstairs, which happened to be in my parents' room. One day, I hung up the phone and turned around and saw a piece of paper sticking out from under the mattress. *What's that trash under there? I need to throw that away. My parents are slobs.* So I ripped it out and (gulp) caught a glance of the most terrifying, confusing images, so... I ripped up the entire mattress and was greeted by a Whitman's sampler collection of *Hustler* magazines. Pretty sure they were not *Playboy*; my dad was not that classy. Something told me I was not supposed to be looking at that stuff. But I couldn't look, and I couldn't look away. The horror of all these naked ladies doing things I could not fathom at the time...

The horror. The horror.

I ran screaming from the room.

Scarred for life.

It took me years to get my head around it.

So then it was my dad in the dirty T-shirt with his arms crossed over a potbelly who explained to me the facts of life while leaning against the kitchen sink, while I stood in the doorway of the kitchen as far away as I could possibly get while still being technically in the room. I looked at him with utter horror as he explained how beautiful and miraculous it all was. This was just gross. This was a *man*, my *father*, telling me these things while I wanted some nice old lady to tell me, like maybe my mother. Where the hell was she? She must've been gardening out in the backyard. Total pruning prude.

I blocked out these uncomfortable memories for over a decade. Or tried to, at least.

By the age of 22, I had heard this term *blow job* on the street in certain contexts and figured it had something to do with the male parts, but my mind would not let me put the word together with what I had seen in those magazines. So one night I was riding around in some car with some guy (still a virgin, of course) obsessing about this issue and I finally blurted out, "I don't get it. *Blow*-job?? You blow? I don't understand how that...*does* anything."

He looks at me and says, "No, you don't blow, you suck." And he cackled.

I wanted to jump out of the car and run far far away like Jenny Gump.

That was what I had seen in those magazines before I had a clue as to what I was seeing. The fog was clearing. I could no longer be in denial. This action would indeed necessitate the penis being *inside* the mouth!!!! It was WAY worse than I thought. Right then I realized that I would never be able to have a man in my life if it meant I had to have a penis in my mouth. *You're going to put what where??!*

And I know you're all thinking. *Oh, this chick's a lesbian.* No, I'm still trapped in hetero hell.

People, is this really normal? Putting mouths on genitals is something only four-legged creatures should be doing, preferably not in polite company.

I guess I have become the total pruning prude my mother was. Even though I hate gardening.

I often wonder how many women actually enjoy doing it. But isn't it pretty much a requirement—basically written into the marriage contract? Isn't the world organized according to blow jobs? *As long as you both shall live, or until she quits giving you head, whichever comes first.*

So as you can see, comprehensive, in-depth sex education might have helped me a great deal in life. Sometimes I wonder if I might've had that if I had gone to a better school. Do private schools have better programs in this subject? I'm thinking they must—everything else is better in a private school, isn't it? At those prices I would assume so, and I would expect that the teachers would take good care of explaining the birds and the bees. And no girls would have to hear about it from their perverted father with the dirty magazines.

After all, it is a jungle out there. And here I am still beating around the bush, so to speak, because a bird in the hand is better than two in the bush. Not sure if that makes any sense, but you get my drift.

Oh, by the way, this story does NOT have a happy ending.

So I still only got the memo about being good at blow jobs to get a guy. I really thought that was all they cared about. I was about 28, I think, when I finally grew the balls to go there. Why don't they offer oral sex as a *class* in college?? We need a safe space where we can practice on dummies—and those mannequins too. Just like CPR. All I know now is that I have not graduated cum loudly because…I can't—or won't— swallow. *That might explain why I am alone now.* When you are in 9th grade and you're with a guy for the first time and he's just telling you that *other* girls have done this with him, how are you supposed to know that he's not lying? Wait. *What other girls?* There is no way to verify what sexual behavior is acceptable, because we usually think certain behaviors are only OK if we know for a fact that most other people do these things, and there is absolutely no way to find out the truth on this. And even that premise doesn't hold water; it just means we are *all* sick, sickos. We are all sex workers. It IS a JOB. A dirty, filthy job. Lack of blowjobs is the leading cause of divorce.

So needless to say, I'm alone now. That is a testament to how good a judge of character I am. See, very few men are *swallow-worthy*. Or even eye contact worthy. Yes. Women are excellent actors. That is what gets us through life.

But at least we don't need to get married or find a sugar daddy or sugar mama just to get *health insurance* anymore. Right? Like we've all been there. Don't lie. Because now we've got Sugarbama. (Or by the time this book comes out, *had* it.) So I took what I used to have to spend on my deductible and went to Hawaii and learned to surf.

Health insurance. That reminds me of the last time I found out I had to go through chemo:

Ok, that's it, I am getting out the bucket list:

#1 Face Lift

#2 Liposuction

#3 Reverse Titanic (without incident)

I mean, I simply cannot start doing high-end traveling before getting everything *fixed*. If I'm gonna stay alive, I wanna look good doing it. And if I'm gonna die, I wanna look good doing that too. That's right. Coming and going. Even at my funeral—I want the open casket with the bikini, dammit, so all the men CRY. "Oh God, it's so tragic. She was still so hot." And the women say out loud, "Wow, I hope I look that good when I'm dead." And the men will all look at each other and size each other up with a look that says, "*You* got to fuck her? Holy shit, what was she thinking? How hard up was she? I am way too good to be in this group of sorry ass motherfuckers. She was just slumming it until she got to me. She finally raised her standards."

So then they try to find out *when* the other guys were with me. I should write a group letter to all the men I've loved.

To all the men I've loved before:

You are all special in your own sweet way. I loved each of you for different reasons and in different seasons of my life. I may have overlapped a few springs and summers, but you know how that goes. No regrets. I only hope that each of you learned something new about the inner workings of the female mind. I know this is a priority for you. And tell your new partner all about me and my book; I am sure she will snap it up on Amazon.

All my exes (sigh)...either I left them, or they killed themselves. So sad when that happens. One of them was in the Heaven's Gate cult. I'm sure you remember that from 1996, or you can just Google it. He was intense and fun and brilliant and darn good in bed, but alas, he was just on break from celibacy. He had been saving up.

Yes. Chemo *"therapy."* Why, it sounds like a trip to the day spa. Some sort of yoga retreat. Nope. It's fuckin' kick-ass poison in your veins. That kind of therapy. There is psychotherapy. There is physical therapy. There is massage therapy. But chemo is not "therapy." There's nothing whatsoever very therapeutic about it, except you do get to sit in a really nice chair. There are some serious high-end chemo chairs out there, like first-class seats on British Airways. All the way to...wherever you happen to be going.

But they don't want you in that chair or that hospital bed very long. *Nurse yelling:* "Do you think you can afford to be in that chair, bitch? That chair costs $5000 an hour, do you understand that? And that bed, don't even get me started on that hospital bed, girl. You git yo ass out of this hospital."

No, I can't afford it, but Sugarbama can... I just figure if you can buy drones, you should be able to pay for a few more hospital beds, and maybe a couple of good schools. I mean...if you've got the money for the one, ya should have the money for the other. One less drone, and a few more hospital beds and two schools that are slightly better...that's what I call killing two birds with one drone.

Let's see. Hospital beds, chairs, and oh yes, hospital gowns—does anyone know how to put one of those on without something hanging out or dragging on the floor? The strings are all over it, but you can't figure out what to do with them—then you finally give up and ask the nurse to help you. This is where the regression to a childlike state begins.

Cancer cells just sit there LTAO as they watch you run on the treadmill, lift weights, eat kale, and execute perfect downdogs. But then the immune system just gets high or lazy and doesn't ask cells for their ID. Or asks, but really doesn't look. *Close the borders! Keep the bad cells out! Build a wall!*

I guess my immune system is just weak on that issue.

See, young people think that folks get old because they *allowed* themselves to get old. Like if someone dies, it's their own damn fault. They think, *Well, if they would just work out and eat kale and avocado toast like us, then they wouldn't die. Such a shame that they just let themselves die like that.*

They look at everyone older and think, *You're all gonna die and I'm not. Ha ha.* Then we get older or have a medical problem and we look around and think, *"None of you understand! I'm gonna die, and you're all gonna live!!!"* Sob.

But I know: none of you out there are ever gonna die because you take the right *supplements.* Yeah, you've done your homework, right? You've researched everything to kingdom come and back again. You know your Resveratrol from your turmeric, don'tcha? So you are absolutely never gonna die. And when something new comes out, you're gonna be all up on that shit too. And don't forget the "adult gummies." You know the ones.

Did you ever get the feeling that you are two people simultaneously? Like one of them is featured in the movie of your life and the other one is doing the running commentary? That one is my Inner 26-year-old and she is just ripping on me. Very harsh critic. But nothing compared to the Inner 12-year-old who is completely let down. Sometimes these two Inner Girls have a conference, and the 53-year-old is not even *invited.* I have to crash the pity party.

They get together and compare the life they thought they were going to get to this *other* life that they didn't see coming, that they just never could have predicted. They are rather... shell-shocked. There's a little PTSD going on because they keep doing this line-by-line analysis and they're like, *Well, this is just not correct. Mistakes have been made.* I blast through the door and tell them straight up that these are certainly not *my* mistakes. Something went awry in the universe. In society. And by the way, what life were you expecting anyway? Fame and riches, a man who worships you, agelessness, world travel? (They look at each other and nod.)

Look, kids, I did everything I thought was right at the time. I mean, I thought I did. So what did I do? What did I not do? What happened? Was that degree in dance really such a detriment? But I was science and math challenged and so were you and we never would have graduated if we had been forced to take those classes. Sad but true. I could have done journalism, but instead I went back and got my English teaching credential. That would maybe get me *A* job, at least. Besides, I was GOOD at dance! You were too! I wanted to do things I was good at. So did both of you! Is that a crime?

And the two Inner Girls unanimously agree that it is not a crime but challenge me by saying *and look, you are still doing it! Even though you could dance naked without any degree at all.* Then I remind them that things could have been SO MUCH worse! I could have wound up in a really *really* bad marriage and had kids on top of it and been trapped in a job I hated. Instead, I am man-free, kid-free, smog-free, financially independent, and living in my lovely cabin in the woods in Michigan. So on balance, even with the cancer crap, things are not all that bad. You have to look at the bigger picture. Get a little perspective.

The two of them look at each other and nod, but have a wistful look on their faces. The 12-year-old says, "But you wanted to be famous. You wanted to be a bestselling author or a movie star or maybe even President!" And the 26-year-old says, "But are you *ever* going to have good sex again? Are you ever gonna have ANY sex again?" And the 53-year-old sighs. Then she stands up straight, lifts her chin, stares them down, and says: *Look. I. Am. Still. Alive... And. Kicking.* And they give her a standing ovation.

The 50 shades of grey are at my mother's church. No, really. I look out over the congregation and that's what I see. I wasn't really going to church, I was just borrowing my mother's church, to make her happy. That's where I met the last guy. He was there apparently hunting for a woman because that's how truly desperate men find women these days (desperate housewives, desperate old guys). But we all do lead lives of quiet desperation—sometimes not so quiet.

Yes, so he fell in love with me, but had no idea how to *prove* it. Blah blah blah, right? At this point, I want the 200K ring or no dice. No interest on my part. Soon after that, I got back in touch with an old flame and fell hard for him. No ring necessary. Not even a tennis bracelet. As if I care about jewelry. But he was not quite ready. Recently divorced. And it will take any divorced guy at least a couple of years to decide if he wants to go through that again. Besides, if a relationship isn't traumatic enough to make me bleed online about it, it's just not worth the time and effort.

Ok, let's lighten things up even more...

My CPA was a real stickler for what I could deduct or not as an entertainer. I wanted to deduct everything I spent at Vic's Secret, and he said, "Well, don't you wear that stuff outside your work?" Fuck no. Why would I wear uncomfortable push-up bras to Costco? I wanted to tell him, "Honey, all the world is a strip club, except the lighting is not always complimentary." That's why boob jobs are not deductible anymore...maybe they were at some point. But they figured, "Hey, sister, you are using those things for both personal and professional functions. You don't *live* at the strip club." Well, I have two boobs, right? So it seems like they would allow you to deduct the cost of one of them— the professional boob, not the personal one. (Just for the record, my boobs are real.) Insert smiley face emoji.

Speaking of my assets, I bought two sports bras today. One of them is called the "full metal jacket" and the other one is called "the booby trap." I kid you not. Did a woman come up with those names? Seems we have kind of gone into the war zone with female sports equipment. Being a woman is pretty much like living in a danger zone. My strategy is to wear the booby trap under the full metal jacket. Nothing is getting through these. I am bullet-proof. Titanium.

Expanding on this subject, I want to know who Victoria is and what's her secret? Is it the lingerie? Because that is not a secret. Was it Queen Victoria? The Victorian age was a time when all the sexy stuff was hidden even though people were extremely active, verging on promiscuous. They knew how to keep a secret. Emily Dickinson could have been a stripper in the 90s, and I could have been Emily had I lived in the mid 1800s. The only difference between me and her is a car and boobs. Well, actually, I never saw her boobs, so maybe it's just the car.

Being a stripper is like being a close cousin once removed to the *idea* of being loved. I mean:

- My skin is showing
- I am close to people
- I am touching people
- People are touching me

- I am showing off

— if that's not love, I don't know what is!

So, yes, I have to integrate all my self-knowledge into my life plan, that's all. Unfortunately, my self-awareness haunts me. But my life plan is not so obvious as other people's boring, linear plans. No, I'm more abstract, improvised, circuitous in my ways...so nuanced that it takes an incredibly incisive person to see into the methods of my madness. I mean, I myself can't even see the methods till much further down the road, because I am taking the scenic route. There is an Inner Guide behind the curtain, and an Inner GPS behind the wheel. But one thing is for sure: Life does not care about logic. Life really is more a matter of instinct and improvisation. It's about being able to do acrobatics when life throws you that curve ball when your crystal ball is in the shop. It's about adapting to circumstances you never could have imagined.

How do I cope? Poetry. Rock and Roll. Mozart. Dancing. Coffee. Trees, mountains, oceans, sky. And looking back at all the acrobatics and realizing that I am a pretty darn good gymnast.

Zero gravity seats. Really? Is there a car seat that lifts your ass? How about zero gravity jeans? I am a genius!

Girls, you know that guy who opens the door for you, listens to you drone on and on, holds your arm as you cross the street, and starts buying you little trinkets a week after meeting you? Don't you just hate that? The first thing you think is he must be desperate or gay. Makes you wanna puke.

Perhaps we women ought to be more careful now that some men are really trying to be warm and sensitive and are allowing themselves to be vulnerable—we shouldn't go off giggling to ourselves that the poor guy is gay or a pussy. Maybe we should start being a little more sensitive to guys' needs. Men are people too! Even white men. Well, that may be going a little too far...

Future book titles:

Angry White Pretty Woman

Hating a Hormone

Running on the Vapors of Youth

The Feminine Mistake

I Just Wanna Look Hot in a Bikini at My Funeral

Good Parenting—By a Kid-Free Agenda-Free Old Lady

How to Like Yourself When Everyone Else Hates You

How to Survive Cancer (and then realize cancer was the least of your problems)

How to Carry On While Not Being a Celeb or a Billionaire

And one cookbook maybe:

The Cookbook of Emotional Eating: What to Eat When Happy, Angry, Sad, Horny

It's not "to be or not to be," but to medicate or meditate? I can't wait for the drone pot drop, and I don't even smoke pot. I have tried a few gummies. I need a pot partner I can trust. Do you ever feel like a mosquito in a cloud of drones?

Okay, fine, I will now entertain technology.

Twitter is kinda creepy. You look at your phone and strangers are following you. So you're constantly looking over your shoulder. There is the retweet and quote tweet and there should be up and down tweets too. Uptweets would raise sexpectations...

So Pinterest the tail on the donkey

thread the needle

upload the needle in the haystack

gigabyte the apple

download the update

tweet retweet and repeat —

Get a virus, go viral, get liked anyway,

but watch my back since I'm being followed?

Well, link me in and beam me up!

Are there iPhones in heaven? Is there a hell for iPhones ? We need more apps for the after-life.

"Digital" — it means you can now do everything with just one finger.

500 channels and my ex-husband watched TV as if he still only had eight. He would just turn it on and watch whatever showed up on the screen—as long as it kept him awake. And get this—he wouldn't even use the info button to find out what he was watching. (Gasp)

When I sit down to watch anything, I'm doing in-depth research. I have to go through every channel and every app every time I tune in, and research all the info on at least five movies or shows. You have to—otherwise you might be missing something really good. And if you don't read the info, how will you ever LEARN anything? And have you ever wondered why they always show shots of the audience reaction on talk shows? Is this in case we can't figure out how to react—we need to see an example?

Beware the hardware, the software, and the firmware;

(these are all terms that came out of the porn industry)

AND

the upgrade,

the update,

the upload, (up yours)

the download, (happens in bathroom)

the kilobyte,

the megabyte,

the gigabyte, (bite me)

the gigahertz, (why not gigahimtz?)

Gigabite my ass!!!

And above all, fear the bundling and the contract. So much sexual innuendo. Tech guys are horny creatures. But there is a contract at the end, after all.

Where do gigabytes come from, and why do we have to PAY for them? Who decided how much a gigabyte costs?? All so we can livestream on Facebook while optimizing our Youtube videos while tweeting to our fan base, and of course posting reviews on Tripadvisor and Amazon. Because I am an *influencer.*

blogging

commenting

following

linking

"friend-ing" (now friend has become a verb)

googling

liking

posting

reviewing

skyping

texting

tubing

twittering: which sounds like what it is—short chirps of gossip from birdbrains

What I never learned about the birds and the bees just kept me beating around the bush—because a bird in the hand is better than two in the bush, but thanks to Twitter I am killing two birds while home alone.

Speaking of birds, I have to admit I did sleep with those damn Angry Birds. Maybe that's not a good way to doze off...with all those exploding birds and pigs. But I've discovered I have an appetite for complete destruction and total annihilation. I close my eyes, and I see the green pig's head teetering on the edge of a concrete block...and I'm turning the iPhone and shaking it like an Etch A Sketch.

People, can we talk?? I'm sorry, please enter your username and password. I believe the iCloud is the leading cause of climate change, seasonal affective disorder, and PTSD.

How's the health of your "online identity"? People have the illusion of connection out there, but all they are really doing is attempting to influence their so-called non-existent "friends" so they can feel like a major online entity soon to go viral. Facebook reminds me of a high school clique that got a little too high and mighty, and then plastered itself all over the cybermap. Now it's just a gang of smarty pants in Silicon Valley, or maybe even a kind of information mafia.

And have you ever actually read any of those "terms and conditions"? The "user agreements"? Information has become a drug, and we are all users. Gigabytes are the new cocaine.

Which device to use?

Who to reach?

How to reach them?

What to communicate?

When to communicate?

Why to communicate? (We don't need a reason.)

Where to send the message?

Keeping in mind that NO ONE wants you to reach them. They have apps and algorithms for you to interface with. That stuff is the new moat surrounding their castle.

jpeg,

pdf,

rtf,

doc,

tif,

gif,

links,

apps,

Where are we going with all this?? No one cares, as long as we just get there *faster*. I just wanna know so I can blog about it...

Blog blog blog...we are getting a bit blogged down here. How much information can any brain actually fucking process?

I think they are coming up with a transdermal wifi patch. They thought about the embedding in clothing idea and thought "no, too tough to deal with body heat and the laundry so...let's just stick it on 'em until we can stick it in 'em." And we all know what happens when something gets stuck in you.

Yes, I have spent many years beating my head against that proverbial brick wall. Why is my head gushing blood? I mean, I have tried sledge-hammers, chain saws, ropes, and crampons, telekinesis, pole vaulting, chiseling, and I have pretty much just wound up with bruises in places I can't talk about and traumatic brain injury. Is it my fault the brick wall is there? And what about that glass ceiling? How do we know it's glass if we can't reach it? If it is glass and I shatter it, the piercing shards will ruin my yoga mat.

If money is fiction, then the 1% is Alice in Wonderland. So I have decided I either wanna be dirt poor or filthy rich—just not on the day I decide to take a shower. Can't think of anything worse to be than middle class—too clean. Why is money so dirty? It needs near constant laundering. I just recycle it via Visa.

It's time to take a damn break, OK? I just need to spend a lot of time lying on my yoga mat gazing up at my reflection in the glass ceiling. Or is it the debt ceiling? I actually did break through that one a few times...and it didn't even hurt. Until later.

Speaking of reflections. Did you ever happen to mention to your "BFF" that you're thinking of getting a certain "procedure" done, and she says, "Oh, you don't need that." So polite! While she's really thinking, *Thank god the hag is finally gonna fix herself.* She doesn't say, "Oh, yeah, definitely time for that...and while you're at it, you might as well get yourself a peel, botox, fill in those lines, and lose the turkey neck. And we just don't have the time to go any further than that."

Because how AM I supposed to get sex if I'm getting old*er*? For some reason, sex is becoming even more important to me as I get older, not less. LIKE AM I EVER GOING TO HAVE SEX AGAIN?? LIKE IS THAT *IT*?! IS THAT THE SUM TOTAL OF MY SEXUAL INTERLUDES *FOR LIFE*??? Yet, because I am older, I trust men even less. I know too much, and it isn't pretty...but I still have to be. Yet as it turns out—pretty is not enough! NO! You also must be able to leap over brick walls and shatter glass ceilings...

But men are just men. They are kind of like rest stops. Loving a man is like loving a picnic table. But how long can you sit at one of those before your ass starts aching? I don't know why I keep expecting them to be better than that somehow, because they honestly just can't help being what they are. It's not their fault they were doused in testosterone in the womb. It's time I gave up hating testosterone, cause that's really all I'm doing by hating men. I am hating a hormone.

So, yeah, hormones. I will admit that I am, officially—post-menopausal. I figure maybe you all won't be so hard on me, knowing that. I mean, it is kind of a disability. *I am hormonally challenged.* And that can be sort of an excuse for this book being all about me. Besides, there's only so long I can pretend to be "interested in others." Let's face it, "others" are boring. They just are. Fuck them. Ah, the joys of misanthropy.

Forget YouTube. It's the MeTube. For every "me" out there who thinks their cat will maintain their online notoriety amongst the cyber community.

Did the Me generation ever really end? Didn't it just morph into *I*pods, *I*phones, and *I*pads? *I* was born right on the cusp of Generation X: 1965. Kind of straddling the generations. So while I was heavily influenced by the Baby Boomers, I am not officially demographically a Baby Boomer. That's why I stand onstage and yap at people, YET I have never smoked pot! I just get high on the sound of my own voice.

And is that so BAD? Is that a SIN? I can think of a lot of other voices I wish never to hear again. I mean, if it's not all about me, who, might I ask, is it about? You? My dog? Obama?? Hillary? Trump?? J.Lo? Taylor Swift? Kim Kardashian? Please. I'm not spoiled, I just *have standards.*

I sometimes do talk to myself just to maintain the illusion that I am still the center of attention. That might be why I am hoarse in the morning.

But seriously, I have to think out loud because I have to hear myself think—or else I get confused. So shut up while I talk to my selves.

But none of my problems are my fault. No.

It's my organic farming commie parents. Oh, yeah, they were aiming for "nonconformist" as they were molding me into their own image, but what they failed to realize was that if they succeeded, that would mean all of their worst fears would come true. So I'm proud of the fact that I haven't held any job for longer than a year—it means I'm successful at being a rebel. Gotta be good at something. I rebel; therefore, I excel at getting expelled, as you can tell, but I'm not in hell because I even rebel against the stereotype of a rebel, you know. I don't go around with tattoos and metal dripping from every appendage and orifice. You could say I'm a rebel in sheep's clothing, since I'm from a farm and all. And I do like wool...

I rebelled against my father:

He told me to go to law school. I majored in dance.

He told me to marry a rich man. I married a poor mechanic.

He told me to have kids. I stayed a kid.

Then I rebelled against my husband:

He went to work. I stayed in bed.

He watched USA. I surfed the net.

He voted Republican. I voted Communi— I mean, Green! I voted Green.

Finally, I rebelled against myself. And here's how that thought process works:

Let's see...

If I make money, I'm failing to rebel against materialism and conformity.

But if I don't make money, I'm an unempowered woman who can't afford to be a rebel.

If I wear heels, I'm failing to rebel against sexism.

But if I don't wear heels, I am failing to rebel against my mother who thinks I'm supposed be "down to earth."

If I drive, I'm failing to rebel against oil companies.

But if I don't drive, I'm failing to rebel against speed limits.

That's how I got where I am today.

Even my ovaries rebelled against me...they knew they would not be needed. So they planned a mutiny...but I'll come back to that.

I know, I know, my problem is I'm over 50 actually—holy cow! And I still don't know what I want to be when I grow up. So I have decided I just won't grow up. I will just live in perpetual perennial adolescence like all the celebs.

Yes, you're right, that's bullshit. I'm already grown up, over the hill, and on a downward trajectory. So I guess it's time I figured out not what I want to be, but what I was...since it's all over, anyway.

So like I said, I majored in *Dance*—thinking that would at least keep me young and thereby buy me more *time* to decide what to do with my life, and in the meantime, I'd be having *fun* doing what I *love*!

I was on the verge of homelessness when I finally figured it out. Swap the leotard for a G-string and get on with it. See, that's marketable. People like that.

I couldn't feel guilty about entertaining men in the only way they underfuckingstand. As long as the playing field is not level, I will use EVERY asset I have to even the odds in my favor. With a little bit of help from Victoria's Secret. Corporate America's policies make poor people poorer, while my policies keep the married men of America from blowing their brains out.

I'll never forget it—when I first started dancing, they told me I needed some sort of *novelty* in my act. Guess what mine was. (Pause) Real boobs. Who knew? It was the 90s after all. I felt a little like Raggedy Ann at a Barbie sleepover. And somehow that feeling has never really left me.

Speaking of Barbie, I guess boys saw their sisters playing with Barbie and they thought, "That's the kind of girl I want: the blonde one with the plastic boobs and legs that go over her head." That's "Fuck Me Barbie." Then they figure out that Barbie is high maintenance and sort of narcissistic. Well, of *course*, look at all the shit she has to do to maintain all that for all these years. That's why she has not had time to get pregnant.

I think there is a pregnant Barbie. It took her awhile to show up. But I can't find a hysterectomy Barbie, or mastectomy Barbie, cancer survivor

Barbie, PTSD Barbie, ADHD Barbie, or God forbid, a *depressed* Barbie. Nope, Barbie hasn't been through shit. I did not own a Barbie when I was a girl. That's my problem in life. Obviously. I had a Raggedy Ann. Organic materials. Cotton. Yarn. Fuck that plastic bitch. To this day I still have floppy boobs, not plastic ones. I'm not really attached to my boobs, but apparently they are attached to me, which is so sweet; they are still hanging around after all this time.

The thing is, now rich bitches are freezing their eggs and they don't have to worry about any deadlines for having kids AND they don't have to go through that horrible disfigurement called pregnancy. That's another job most American women don't want to do. We can farm out *everything*. Freeze the eggs, buy the sperm, hire the uterus. And nine months later, you get a baby you can leave at home with the nanny. Beautiful.

And did you know that Barbie was originally based on a German doll called Lilli, a prostitute gag gift handed out at bachelor parties? So there you have it, Barbie got her start at bachelor parties. No surprise there.

Now I do realize that the course of my life has been kinda sorta determined by my boobs, since I did meet my first husband at "the club." He was kind of a diamond in the rough. About a half carat. I'm not much into carats though, I'm more of a celery kind of girl. Not salary. No, I am more vegan than that.

It was completely ironic. His auto shop was across the street from the club and everyone knew it, but of course, we lied to everyone about how we met.

"Sooo, how did you two meet?"

"Well, I was, um, in the neighborhood, and I, uh, needed an oil change. I was also kinda hungry, so I went down to the corner deli and asked the guy if he knew any honest mechanics in the area. He directed me straight to my future husband's shop. So I brought my car in, and we got to talking, and one thing led to another, and the rest is history!"

I think they bought it.

So I'm here to tell you that old topless dancers don't die. They just marry mechanics and move to Orange County.

I still don't understand why anybody would be in a hurry to be an adult. I mean—what does it get you?

Bills, in-laws, kids, mortgages, kissing ass.

Home improvement, insurance, teenage kids, taxes, kissing ass.

Heart burn, heart disease, cancer, depression, osteoporosis, sex changes, divorce, kissing ass.

Death. And probably a LOT more kissing ass after that. I'm a liberal, after all. I'm going to hell unless I repent pretty damn quick!

I keep trying to find Jesus. I have looked everywhere for this individual, but he's not on Facebook, and Google can't find him. I find it pretty hard to believe in someone who's not even online. Oh, you believe in God? That's okay, I forgive you.

Seriously, though, the older you get, the more respect you have for dead people because these people will eventually be your neighbors. I really wonder how they do the zoning in the great map of the afterlife. I hope there's GPS in heaven, because I don't want to make a wrong turn and wind up...oh, wait, there are no bad neighborhoods in heaven.

Now that I think of it, I really have been fired from every job I ever had. Yeah. I lost my jobs like a real man: I got fired. I am not a quitter. Of course, one of those times was when the cute guy from the gym stopped by the deli where I was working one summer after college and we exchanged longing stares over the tabouli and veggie burgers. Then I got fired for not wrapping up the cheese. So that was his fault. Not mine.

But mostly I get fired because I refuse to act like a moron and work amongst real morons. Like I would be the one who would stand there and say, "Why are you doing it that way?" I just can't stomach being part of a substandard system. You know, though, by being lazy, or at least indecisive, I am actually creating jobs. By *not* doing stuff, I'm creating opportunity for someone else to do it! I am so good for the economy that way.

And so I, like so many other "ordinary Americans," manage "money" by shrewdly shifting my credit card balances from one card to another... and another...and another. It's like recycling money over and over and over. That is environmentally sound financial management if I do say so myself. Paperless!

So after I quit dancing, I found out what non-dancers do for money. They get up in THE MORNING and drive to a JOB, EVERY FUCKING DAY!!

So I tried getting real, and I became a teacher. But they kept letting all these KIDS into my room. I don't see how I'm supposed to concentrate with all those kids in there. I mean, they're talking, breathing—they're in my Line of Sight! That's just a HUGE distraction. Because you see, I have a touch of ADD, and my doctor says it would be best for everyone if every so often I stayed in a sensory deprivation chamber. Like the one I'm in right now. How do you expect me to get anything done?

ADD...so many Ds out there these days.

3-D

OCD

ADHD

DVD

HD

LCD

LED

ACDC (Rock on)

and then the DD, which of course leads to the STD.

To make matters worse, one of the girls in my class told me I looked like a "milf." I had to look it up at the time. Shit. *That's* what I looked like to those teenage boys?! No wonder.

So one year I was teaching at a girls orthodox Jewish school. Sort of like the Vegas singer hiding out in a convent. I thought I'd be safe there. And I told one of these Jewish girls that I was from a farm, and she gazed at me with sympathy and said, "That's okay." I just felt so much better about myself after that.

Speaking of school, there's that ugly phrase: "Do the math." I honestly can't do the math. It is depressing. If I try to do *the math*, I will realize that I should have tried harder in my ninth grade algebra class. But I had the most awful teachers in high school, so again, not my fault. Yeah, I want to be a seventh grader again, so I went to an open house for seventh grade and told them I wanted to start over again with seventh grade math because that's where I started to lose it. I fucked up with those stupid fractions, so I want a do-over. I need some decent teachers this time and learn the goddamn fractions, and then I can finally go to Harvard by the time I am maybe 55.

After working in both a school and a strip club, I have to say I feel safer in the strip club than the school. Especially lately. People are pretty much happy in a strip club, but someone out there knows that schools, on the other hand, are indoctrination factories and need to be stopped. Brainwashing stops when an AK-47 shows up.

Let's go domestic here, shall we?

I haven't cleaned my shower in so long even the mildew has a website. And those spiders are the ultimate website builders, aren't they? After I work out, I use my damp socks to dust with. Saves water.

I get the dust off pictures by dragging them across my ass. That is how you do that, right? I used to redecorate my husband's bathroom by repositioning the economy-size can of Planter's cashews.

My second husband insisted on doing the laundry as soon as it hit the hamper, but I think that a hamper is like a vacation for clothes. They get a chance to just sit there and be wrinkled and dirty and no one cares. They don't have go out and impress anybody. They don't have to hang around waiting for their turn to get out of the closet. They need time to themselves. And have you ever gone through your closet and found clothes you don't even want your mother to see you in? Sometimes I think I'm a closet lesbian, based on what I find in my closet.

My ex-boyfriend in Colorado was anal about loading the dishwasher. I would put stuff in, and he would take it out and rearrange it. I could not meet his exacting standards. He was a much better cook than I was too. He could make jambalaya. I did not even know what jambalaya was.

My ex-fiancé had a Roomba *and* a Black and Decker dust buster. *What?* I have a broom and a mop. And I only use them when I can't stand looking at the cobwebs that are at eye level when I am in down dog.

Kitchens are where slaves work. They are well disguised slaves' quarters, no matter how modern they are. Even the gilded cage is still a cage. So I don't have one. What really knocks me out is these one-percenters who have kitchens bigger than my gym and where you can't discern the cabinetry from the refrigerator and you can actually have a conversation with the appliances—and then they go out to eat. It's all just for show when they entertain twice a year.

The reason women do all the work in the home and most of the important work outside the home is because men suck at *all* of it. We would do everything if we only had the time, because we know we would do it better. So we women had a meeting and we decided to give men very specific technical jobs so that we could get on with managing the bigger picture.

Speaking of cleaning house, my boyfriend and I broke up. (Sigh) Again. But this time we are being so mature about it we can even still have sex once in a while…no biggie. It was a mutual agreement, you know, just helping each other out through the dry spell that usually ensues after such a rendering. We are growing up, I would say. We might even become mature adults someday. We have kinda been kickin' the can down the road on that one…little bit. But, hey, no harm in that, right? What else is the road for but kicking cans?

Roads. That brings me to…transportation: Sport. Utility. Vehicle. Is commuting a utility or a sport? I think both. Getting groceries is an expedition? Are you really gonna fill that whole thing up with crap from Walmart?? Are there any paths left to find? Lands left to rove? Trails left to blaze? Of course! So we have:

The Discovery

The Endeavor

The Highlander

The Pathfinder

The Trailblazer

For meet-ups:

The Rendezvous

The Envoy

The nod to the natives:

The Grand Cherokee

The Aztec

Move over Range Rover, we've got:

The Land Rover

The Land Cruiser

And the Freelander

For Alaska rovers:

The Avalanche

The Yukon

The Denali

For Army guys:

The Trooper

The thinking man's SUV:

The Axiom

The Element

The Touareg??

For rappers:

The Escalade

The Escape

The Excursion

The Expedition

The Explorer

The Xterra

Then we "Go west, young man":

The Pacifica

The Sequoia

The Tahoe

The Durango

And for those whose other car is a private jet:

The Aviator

The Pilot

The Hummer (which should give you an orgasm as you drive over the speed bumps also known as Mini Coopers and Honda Fits)

Moving on to the spice rack line: The Cayenne (what's next, paprika?) Chefs will name cars! The Rosemary! The Cilantro!

I think Ford should develop a line of Presidential SUVs. They could make one called "the Bushwhacker," with built-in brush-clearing equipment.

Or The Reagan—Teflon coated, costs $50,000, and gets 5 mpg.

Or The Carter—runs on peanuts.

The Clinton—GPS comes pre-loaded with directions to all McDonald's, trunk loaded with clean dresses. It feels your pain, though.

The Obama car—You hope it starts?

And that leads me to dieting:

I'm on the "servings per package" diet. That's the one when you just start eating right from the box and keep eating and eating, and then you look at the servings per package info, and then you figure out how many calories are in the WHOLE thing, and then you estimate how much of the package you already ate. That's how I "do the math."

Did you ever wonder what the solution to every problem is? CHOCOLATE!! Every time, everywhere, it just makes it easier to get through.

Cancer? Chocolate!

Divorce? Chocolate!

Job loss? Chocolate!

Self-sabotage? Chocolate!

Aging? Chocolate!

Depression? Chocolate!

Weight gain? Chocolate!

War? Chocolate!

Terrorist attack? Chocolate for that too, for sure.

So imagine my horror when Hershey's started actually taking some of the chocolate OUT and replacing it with air! Someone put air in the chocolate, and they still want me to pay the same price that I do for chocolate without air in it? If I wanted to buy air, I'd call NPR. Leave the chocolate IN the chocolate. I think Hershey's is getting a little too full of itself to get away with that stunt.

At least I don't have kids begging me to buy the airhole chocolate. Yeah, they gave me a choice: Would you like the cancer or the kids? I did a quick cost-benefit analysis and decided that the cancer would be cheaper and ultimately less hazardous to my health.

Hmm, maybe I should adopt a tiger to sub for the kids.

I think it's great, though. Women are coming out and telling their stories:

"I had a mastectomy."

"I froze my eggs."

"I had ovarian cancer."

"I am a woman trapped in a man's body."

"I had to watch Louis C. K. masturbate."

There will be two kinds of kids in the future: the "fresh" and the "frozen," now that many women are putting their eggs on ice. That might result in a new pecking order in school: "You came from a frozen egg, didn't you?"

I think I will just start buying eggs and sperm and designing people myself. So I found a sperm bank when I googled "buying sperm." And then I found this blog for single women who want to have a child, but can't or haven't yet, for whatever reason. Here are some of the reasons the website lists as to why a woman would want to do this:

- I am sick of living my life for myself, i.e. clothes, jewelry, facials, massages etc. (I do not buy this for a second.)

- I love spending time with my niece and nephew, i.e. playground, zoo, reading books, bathing, feeding etc. (Yes, and then giving them back.)

- I am scared of getting old and being alone. (You will grow old alone just like everyone else. There is no guarantee that any kid will be around for you later in life.)

- I have so much love to give, but no child to give it to. (You can give love to anyone, honey.)

- I want the mother-child bond; I want to feel needed. (The world needs you.)

- I hate holidays, get-togethers etc. because I am the only one without a child. (Embrace yourself. Or just stay home.)

- I feel weird not having my own family and feel like the perpetual child showing up to family gatherings. (What is better than being a child? An adult is nothing more than an experienced child.)

- I am finding it harder and harder to connect with people since I am childless. (Find new friends and new passions.)

- I am envious of mothers. (They are envious of you.)

- I became depressed when thinking that I would not have children. (As opposed to postpartum depression?)

- Having a child would make my life rich and meaningful. (Only YOU can make your life meaningful.)

- I now have time, money, patience, and feel that I can provide a good life for a child. (And then you would have no more time, money, or patience for anything else.)

- I want a home with toys, love, chaos, and a swing set. (You don't need kids for a swing set, toys, and chaos. Look at me.)
- I am sick of having no responsibilities! (Be responsible for the world.)

Did you ever hear anyone say, "Wow, I am *so glad* I have the responsibilities I have"?

It's amazing how persuasive this site feels it has to be to make the women feel like they are in the right place. Guessing it's because they find out how expensive it is. But you would assume that they don't need all this persuasion if they found the site in the first place. And that they have money to burn. Anyone who has kids or thinks of having kids has money to burn or thinks they will.

So who the heck is Tom Brady?? Tim Tebow? Oh, yes, football...aka the national religion. My country, 'tis of the saints and the patriots. Speaking of patriots, I found it very telling that all they could come with in 2012 to beat the Black man in the oval office was a goofy-looking group of sad-sack white boys. And that is STILL all they had to put up against Hillary, except for one Black man, one Fiorina, and one Hispanic. Politics is a sport, after all; that's why you have to RUN for office, and that's why they make you pick sides. Now, the other Black men I see on TV playing sports are running and jumping and sweating their balls off. The white guys are gonna have to do better than hand gestures. They all need some serious athletic training, starting with boot camp.

And golf is not a sport. Unless you are Tiger Woods, I suppose. But mostly, golf courses are just pastures for Baby Boomers.

I wanted to come up with some thoughts about the whole lap dancing thing. You know, what a guy thinks while he's getting a lap dance... what a stripper thinks while performing a lap dance...what a guy thinks while on the tip rail...what a stripper thinks while on the pole...and I realized it's all the same answer: NOTHING. There's no THINKING going on in a strip club. That's the whole point. You go there for the same reason you go to any bar: to stop thinking.

But seriously, exotic entertainers are shrewd businesswomen. We can size up a guy in all ways in about 2 seconds flat. And this notion that strippers, and generally most women, are "gold diggers" is the most anti-women kind of thinking there is out there. What should we be digging for? Rusty nails? Aluminum cans? Lost change on the beach? No MAN would dig for anything but gold. But men seem to care more about beauty than money in their mate/date, as if their wealth is reflected in how hot their wife is. Women are not as concerned with looks in the man, because it is not a practical thing. Looks fade. Money lasts. This should lead one to believe that men are superficial and women are the practical ones, not the other way around.

But wait! There's more!

We are all trying to turn back the clocks, and I am running on the vapors of youth. I save my money for surgery—either to save my life, save my ass, or save face.

Did you ever wonder why "The Price is Right" is always on TV at the doctor's office?

You know you're older when you start dates by comparing what you put in your protein shake.

You know you're older when you go to the mall and wonder *What are all these kids doing here?*

You know you're old when you can't remember where the mall is.

You know you're older when you want to go to the gym when no one else is there.

You know you're old when you can't remember why you ever went to the gym.

You know you're older when entertainment for you is lighting a candle and listening to music from the 90s.

You know you're old when entertainment is a crossword puzzle in a Craftmatic bed.

You know you're older when you only want to travel to really warm places.

You know you're old when you'd rather not fly.

You know you're older when chocolate sounds better than sex.

You know you're old when you haven't even thought about sex since the 90s.

I don't really like it when people "mix up" the sex and the violence. I know it's trendy and all, but I kinda like my sex separate from my violence. Planned out for different days of the week. I'm big on organization like that...and alcohol with books but not with sex. Now some people like to put drugs and sex together too, but it seems like that must mean that neither one is really good enough to stand on its own...if you have to combine like that.

Craps. I mean, the name is filthy to begin with, and way too much coming on the table. That is a filthy dirty game.

So Vegas was pretty much built due to the mafia's need for a place to launder their money, and Joey said, "How about the middle of the fuckin' desert?" Hey!

What is it with women in Vegas and the shoes? They have to wear like—trendy boots to Target on a Friday night. I know she's just picking up some last-minute items on her way to the *club*, but...I just love being at Target in my purple Walmart sweatpants on a Friday night. (Sigh) So peaceful. I'm just looking for a really firm—broom. There are a lot of wimpy ass brooms out there. I need one with the good stiff… whisker thingies.

Absence makes the heart grow fonder? No! Absence makes the penis wander. Money makes the world go round, and it also makes the girl go down.

I am on my own at this point because I know my knight in shining armor is not going to show up to save my ass because my ass is too far gone to be saved. And even if he did show up, I would not recognize him because by this time he has gotten a bit wrinkled and flabby himself. If I did recognize him, I would just yell at him for being so fucking late! Then he'd give me some lame ass excuse, and proceed to pay more attention to his horse and polishing his armor.

"Why do you want all those degrees? All they're good for is teaching."
Yeah, teaching. What's that about?

"I don't want my kids learnin' nothin' 'cept addin' an subtractin' and learnin' to text from the textbook. And of course Jesus too."

You know that quote by Mark Twain about how a lie travels at light speed while the truth puts its boots on. It has to wear boots; it's getting deep out there. Lies just keep rolling around in the mud. They don't care how dirty they get. Now, usually I just lie in bed because that is not a place where you want to be telling the truth.

Let's see then. I've been fired from almost every job I ever had, Hollywood rejected me, the schools rejected me, I even got rejected from a suicide cult. Who does that happen to? I have turned rejection into an art form. At least I beat my ex-husbands to the punch and left them first. Otherwise, I just have a total knack for being completely unacceptable to just about everyone. To me, it must mean I'm doing everything right in life. It's not that I don't know how to play the game; it's that I don't even want to learn, because we all know it's rigged and slanted towards those with advantage, and those who buy into (literally) the whole capitalist mindfuck. That's my excuse, anyway. To paraphrase the lines from *Working Girl:* Who wants to spend their lives beating themselves up and getting nowhere just because they followed bullshit rules made by somebody else (men)?

And I wouldn't want to be with any guy who would want to be with me. "You want *me?* Okay, what's wrong with *you?*" And chances are he just doesn't know me very well yet. Or he's just lying. To himself.

I went back to LA from Michigan about 5 times over the years. I stayed in California until I either went broke, got divorced, or got cancer. The second time I went back I had saved up $5000. Yes! That's enough! And a slightly used car w/ AC! That's how much I hated the Midwest. I would leave it before I was really prepared to leave it. Who is ever really prepared? For anything?

I came back one time after about 7 years in SoCal, and I went to a little gathering in Chicago and I noticed all the people there were talking about all kinds of high-end subjects and I just thought, *Wow, these people are really smart.* And then I realized *No. I am stupid. They're just average intelligence.* The California sun fries your brain cells, and everybody is just going to the gym, getting a tan, getting Botox, and figuring out who to screw to get their next role. That's pretty much it. Not a whole lot of cultural or intellectual stimulation.

See, they don't really give anybody a step-by-step guide on what to do if you want to be an actress or any sort of an artist/musician/writer/singer/comedian/whatever. Nobody really breaks it down for you. Step one, step two, step three…you know, specific, all laid out. Nope. It's fly by the seat of your pants. Improvisation. That's why the only four things they do tell you to do is go to LA or NYC, get your headshots done, take improv classes, and get an agent. That's it. Those four little things involve a lot of other little steps that can literally take years.

- How do I survive in these cities?
- Where exactly do I live?
- How much will it cost?
- Where do I find a decent photographer?
- How do I take good pics?

- How much do improv classes cost?
- Where do I find good ones?
- What if everyone in the class hates me?
- How do I get an agent?
- How long will it be til I make any money?
- What about getting into the union?
- Who wants to hang out with a struggling artist/dancer/writer/ actress?

Damn it! Who the fuck told me it would be a good idea to get into this business? Oh, yeah. Nobody did. Everyone told me not to. I just thought it would be fun and challenging. And I had no idea how challenging. It really is just for rich people's kids.

PART III
Pushing the Envelope

If you have read this far, you must be a glutton for punishment. So let's talk more about this cancer stuff, because it's getting so common these days that whenever you happen to tell someone that you had cancer, they say, "Oh, yeah? What kind did you have? I had blah blah blah," and then they launch into talking about their *own* cancer. Or they tell you about a friend or family member who died from it. Good times. Let's talk about it.

I had been shopping at discountstripper.com looking for 8-inch platform heels, and a few weeks later, found myself at discountsurgical.com looking for compression stockings.

I've never been a soldier at war, but I feel like going through cancer is like going off to war and coming home and no one even wants to acknowledge that they ever knew you. You feel abandoned and unlovable. It's as if you aren't who you used to be at all, as if that person is dead and there's this sorry substitute in her place. So there is a long period of rebuilding and you usually have to reinvent your entire social network from scratch (all the while wondering what the point is), and rebuild any relationship you may have had with any family members because you tend to take things out on them when you think you're *dying*. It's also painstaking to start all over again in any professional line of work, because you are dealing with the loss of part of your identity and most likely some gap in your working life. I did anyway. And on top of that, I was underemployed or self-employed to begin with, all three times I went through it. Struggling plus cancer = ?? That's just one more equation I can't solve. You rethink your goals and deal with a tsunami of self-doubt and guilt. You feel like everyone has passed you up in the rat race. Then you start to question the race. What is the point? More money? So what? (Of course, a cancer diagnosis is not necessary for any of this kind of fall-out.)

Yet, it is only at this point that you can begin to figure things out. Figure out how your whole point of view might have been highjacked by media and social influences. And finally, maybe, after you dig deeper, you figure out *that one thing*, even though it seems impossible to even think.

Speaking of things, does someone have my tumors? Are they in a tumor bank somewhere? Tumors must be worth something if they are putting them in *a bank*. Just like sperm. They want a piece of me? They should pay me. I am not just *giving away* my body to science. I'm not that philanthropic. There has to be a way to figure the value of a tumor. And mine is super rare, so... I should definitely look into this.

A few lucky guesses are the only reason I'm still alive. It's ovarian, but it's a certain type that accounts for only 2% of all the ovarian cancers out there. I'm very distinctive even in my choice of diseases. This thing has my personality written all over it. See, it's called "indolent," which is like a mix of docile, latent, indigent, and indulgent.

It all started when I was 30 in 1996 (yes, it has been 23 years), and I felt this lightning bolt stab me in my lower gut. They took a look with the ultrasound and told me my right ovary was "bad" and needed to come out. Well, I thought, *That's bullshit. Nobody's gonna take a piece of me.* So I ran out of there and thought, *Oh, fuck. Well—I don't have any damn health insurance.* So I just… waited around till the thing just blew up. And then it was appendicitis-type pain, and I ran screaming to the clinic and told them to put me out of my misery. Yes, emergency surgery is just the best. There you are eating grapes in the morning having no clue you're going to be on the operating table in the afternoon. So there's the stomach tube down the gullet and one up the nose too. And that's sheer joy when they rip that thing out later.

So like I said, the thing ruptured, right? Well, that means things kind of spilled out into the bowl down there, so now there's this residual mess that they could not exactly clean up. It's not like you can take a fucking vacuum cleaner to suck out cancer cells. It's not like liposuction. I wish. She just took the right ovary and tube and left the other side since it looked okay and I was only 30 and was still supposed to have kids. I told her later that I did not think I would, but she was just, "Oh, sure you will."

When she told me what it was, all I heard was "a low-grade blah blah blah yada yada yada." My ears did not hear "tumor" or "cancer." My brain stopped reception after the word "low-grade." She did not mention the word "oncologist" to me or tell me to get check-ups more often—just do the annual routine. So I thought, "Okay, it's over. It was just some fluke that will never happen again." I healed up, forgot all about it, and went right back to my type-A lifestyle, even skipped the broccoli.

After I moved to California and got a new gynecologist and filled out that detestable medical history form, I recalled that thing as being "benign." Really, that's what I honestly remembered. Two years had passed by then. I went about my business for about 4 years and ignored my erratic periods and periodic hyper-bleeding, and barely noticed when my periods actually ceased altogether. When I finally did take note, I decided that the left ovary just got "tired" and it knew there was no point in carrying on with all that ovulating hogwash because it was clear that fertility in me was an exercise in futility.

When I finally went in for my annual exam and informed her of these events, she poked around, found the cause of these symptoms, and sent me for an ultrasound. She told me to find my surgical report from the "benign" ovary problem. Oh, that thing? I had no idea where the hell that was. I was probably the most in-denial patient she had ever had. I mean, I was immortal back then.

I honestly had believed I was invincible up until that point. I mean, I ate healthy, mostly *organic*, I was an athlete, didn't smoke or drink, lived near the beach. Yes, all that. Even did yoga. But this time...well, they found two tumors, and where there are two tumors there are probably more scattered around the local vicinity. Yes, they found this stuff basically having a party down there.

My husband at the time had not signed on for this. We already had significant communication problems (we never talked) before the cancer, and then when it came along, it was too much. He became a spectral figure, just wafting in and out with hardly a look or a word. And forget about spooning or cuddling. Can't do that with a ghost. Living with someone you thought loved you and then going through something like that and realizing that person does not actually love you, is a special kind of solitary confinement. It's like an invisible wall now exists between you and that person. You can see the life you had, but you cannot be part of it anymore. You cannot reach it. You cannot touch it. It's like a train leaving the station and you missed it. You had a ticket and you spent all the money you had on that ticket.

After two years of recovery, I was ready to move on—which meant a divorce and moving back to Michigan. I just didn't feel like I wanted to pay rent all over again, much less doing crappy work to make rent.

Besides, I was almost 40.

So that was all in 2003.

Then it made a comeback in 2013. Are you fucking kidding me?!

I have gotten used to calling it my once a decade mechanical internal cleansing. Sort of like my "corporate restructuring."

The 2013 disruption happened while I was living alone in a house I had just bought in Vegas. It also forced me to realize that all that moving around and working in cold industries resulted in my having *no friends*, certainly no man, and then what do I do about *this body*? After recovering from the surgery, the chemo, the hormone treatment,

I had to get back up and try to rebuild my life *again,* and that always starts with my body. And then adjusting to a life without a man or men. After all, all that cancer and the treatment affects certain things. The joke was on me, as I had always had a man in my life and was fairly certain I always would.

Despite this underlying assumption, I only looked for a man periodically—not constantly, not consistently, and certainly not systematically. I knew my true loves were words, music, and the landscape. My life increasingly became more about me becoming more me, rather than figuring out how to alter myself to suit someone else. But I wanted to love. And to be loved. In spite of being me and *because* of it.

Really, it's so simple though, and all women want to do is complicate it. A domestic relationship is about fucking, eating, and fixing stuff. But I always wanted choirs singing, angels weeping, thunder rolling, horses stampeding, tales of woe and anguish, trips around the world on private jets, fights and make-up sex at the top of Mt. Everest, the Kama Sutra during a train ride across France...But really, it's just about fucking, eating, and fixing things. Maybe building a deck. Maybe finishing the basement. That's about it.

(Geez. I just realized why men fish: the fishing pole is an extension of the penis. I don't see very many women fishing, at least not for fish.)

Yeah. Where are the highs and lows? Where are the orgasmic breathtaking over-the-top declarations of undying love and devotion? What? Is that all you want? Please. That is not going to pay the rent or buy a house or send the kids to the finest schools. Oh, wait. I don't have any kids. Well, there's that house thing. Well, shit, just get yourself a fixer-upper and be done. Someday.

So then the topic of religion inevitably comes up when one is dealing with the concept of their mortality. But not for me! I don't practice that stuff. Yet, I have realized that I am a god damn Christian, dammit! I am a bigger Christian than all of you churchgoers out there.

Here's why:

I do not feel the need to show off my car every Sunday.

I feel guilty about my carbon footprint. Or handprint.

I do not feel the need to show off a new outfit, purse, or shoes every Sunday.

I feel guilty when I throw food away.

I feel guilty if I don't recycle.

I will care about the same things I care about now even after I am dead.

I do not believe anyone or anything can "save" me.

I stay busy devising ways to leave an indelible mark on civilization. Like Jesus did.

I do what Jesus did.

Start a revolution.

Tip over some tables.

Say some shocking things.

No one in church is doing what Jesus did.

Edgy comedians and rock stars are more like Jesus than anyone at church, for sure.

First it's about where you are. Then it's all about what you're doing. And at last it's only about who you're with, because you realize that no matter who you are, where you are, or what you are doing, *you can't do it alone.* Except you can die alone, if that's all you are up to.

There I was: post-cancer, unemployed, alone. The lowest hanging fruit, so to speak, was always to just head back to the strip club for immediate financial catch-up, and then go from there. Or try to, anyway. Or not.

Strippers' deals with themselves:

I'm only going to do this until...

My credit cards are paid off.

I'm done with nursing school.

My car is paid off.

I can pay for my facelift.

I can pay for my boob job.

I pay off my student loans.

I get the down payment for my house.

My house is paid off.

I meet the love of my life.

I can pay for my vacation.

I don't make any money anymore.

I'm dead.

I like to think I am the Thinking Man's Stripper.

It's now 2015, and I'm sitting in my 2007 Prius with 213,000 miles on it, outside of Walgreens in Kalamazoo at the age of 50 waiting for what I think is a break-up call. Numbers are a bitch. They tell a story all by themselves sometimes. I am running out of time, and my car is running out of miles.

Listen to your body!

Ovaries: "God, this is boring down here. What are we doing all this for? Let's go on strike. Let's do something she can't ignore!"

Vagina: I need some mouth-to-mouth resuscitation.

Boobs: Do not compare us to Barbie boobs. Or we will kill you.

Feet: How many more times are you going to shove nails up our ass?

Let's review.

The men I have loved:

The Mountain Man

The Cultist

The Abortionist

The Truck Driver

The Socialist

The Frat Boy

The Tom Cruise Wannabe

The Martyr Mechanic

The Terrorist Next Door

The Farm Boy/Salesman

The Tall Guy with the One Eye

The Rotund Overeducated Underachiever

The Short Geek

The Pothead

The Aloof Ph.D.

(No offense, you guys. This is humor. I know you are laughing.)

Insecurity:

As an immigrant, I would never get into this country.

I don't have a Ph.D.

I don't have millions.

I don't have medical training.

I am not an engineer.

I am not a scientist.

I have no children.

I don't speak five languages.

The bar is set pretty high for those who were not lucky enough to be born American, who can be as stupid and undeserving as they want and not get deported.

Yes, it's so fun to go into a new doctor's office and they treat you like you're a complete idiot and have no clue about your own health or medical history. They act like you don't know that you're supposed to exercise and you don't know how to do squats. Here I am a college-educated former dancer, English teacher, personal trainer, exotic entertainer, actress, and cancer survivor, but they only see a rural middle-aged dumb woman. After I jokingly complain about putting on weight, the 26-year-old nurse practitioner flips her long hair and says, "Why don't you just go to the gym?"

Wow. Why didn't I think of that? Your day will come, sweetie.

Then there was the experiment of sending my resume into one of those resume doctors who check the vitals on the thing and tell you it's DOA. I emailed her back regarding her evaluation and told her straight up I had been out of the job market for 15 years, I was a three-time cancer survivor, and I was lucky to still be a bankable asset in the strip club. (Actually, it's not luck. It is pure unadulterated drive to survive in spite of everything.)

I did not hear back from her.

Think about it. Pretty much all women, not just those with cancer, get

poked

scraped,

scoped,

scanned,

prodded,

cut,

squeezed,

dyed,

injected,

waxed,

peeled,

sanded,

painted,

lasered,

and fucked.

So you find out you have cancer. What's the first thing that comes to mind after that? Your family? No, fuck them. It's your own survival. It's your prognosis. It's: *How long have I got? How much time am I gonna lose to this? What are my treatment options? What are the side effects of these options? What am I gonna look like and feel like after this is over? And will it ever BE over?*

It's your body—you know, that thing you have been carting around, or rather, the thing that has carted you around for decades. That's the horse. You are the cart. The "you" that is housed within your body, but is somehow not just your body, but without your body "you" would be homeless. A person without a body does not exist. So, yes—WE ARE OUR BODY!!

You start thinking, *Well, my heart's OK, right? I don't have diabetes. I still have my boobs— that's a biggie. I don't have lung cancer. I don't have myeloma. At least it's not pancreatic, for crying out loud. No leukemia. I'm not in pain. I can still eliminate. I still have my limbs. I can still control my limbs. I can see. I can hear. I can talk. My brain still works. To an extent.* You know you've hit rock bottom when you're counting the diseases that you *don't* have and the parts of your body that are still working.

Then you might think about your family, but if you're like me, you are divorced with no kids and all you have are siblings who are circling like vultures. I didn't choose that. Did you pick your family of origin? And then you start to think that maybe you were stupid not to have kids because your own parents are dead and you figure that if you had children those children would be on your side. They would actually *love* you. Maybe.

Then you think, *Okay, I am going to live for today, dammit!* I am going to stop planning and start living. Because short-term plans are the plans that have a greater chance of happening.

Long term = long time. No urgency.

Short term = short time. That's a deadline.

Forget long-term plans because there is never a way to see far enough down the line to have a 10-year projection. What?

What a ridiculous interview question. *Where do you see yourself in 10 years?* On a beach in the South Pacific, I would hope. Five years is still too far out. One year is about right. But try to live as many days as possible as if they are your last. Because you just never know, right? Life is uncertain, so keep eating nothing but Krispy Kremes. And also try to squeeze as many days as possible into one day. *No, that is a recipe for disaster. What would happen if everyone did that? We would all be doing insane things every day. Eating a whole chocolate cake, skydiving, riding roller coasters, blowing off people on social media…hmm, I guess lots of people do live like they are dying.*

All my life I thought my biggest problem was money. Maybe. But the biggest *distraction* was men. It was the search for Mr. Big and the Big O. And all of this got in my way of finding true fulfillment that I alone owned.

Take it easy, I'm just chatting amongst my selves.

You really have to feel sorry for men, though. Straight white guys, anyway. They live in such prisons. They *have* to fuck something, they *have* to make a bunch of money (or at least more than their friends), they *have* to watch sports. They *are* their paycheck. Thank god women don't have to deal with those bullshit imperatives. We can just go buy a boob job if we feel the need to improve our status. That doesn't cost that much. Cheaper than college. We *are* our image.

Women are still what men say we are. We are fighting this, but it's a tough battle. Still categorized according to looks. Perhaps you are thinking, *Oh, no, the patriarchy is dying off or finally waking up, and women are whatever they decide they are.* If a high-status, high-profile male passes judgment on any particular woman, even if she is high status too, she will have a hard time shaking off that comment.

I sometimes think there really are just two classes of people: readers and non-readers. Thinkers and non-thinkers. There's a reason why classes are called "classes." That's where class is instilled or injected. Maybe. As opposed to prisons, which is where all the fun trends start:

- anal sex

- tats

- flip-flops

- homosexuality

- bleaching assholes

Trust me, you will want to look good for your surgery so they will want to save your life. They do better work on good-looking people. Truly. And the nurses can admire your hair and makeup while you are on the operating table. Think of it: They are putting your rag-doll non-sentient body on a TABLE like a frog to dissect in science class, carving you into manageable pieces. Pull up a chair! Better yet, let's do this in a stadium theater and charge admission.

They are going to take out organs, move them around, scoop out gunk, scrape, poke and prod, then put you back together, stitch you up, and send you home to suffer—alone.

Then you spend many *long* hours doing stuff like writing what you think everyone will want to read. Someday.

Is there a short hour? I know the long hours are when time does not fly but rather seems to creep along like a snail after a couple of vodka martinis, or a fly stuck in a windowsill all winter. The short hours are when you are in a glider over the Rockies. Or when you are sailing the Riviera. Or cruising the Inside Passage. Or actually having sex!!! I know that's just minutes. Short minutes. There are short minutes and long minutes. That's a whole other dimension.

Like most people, I always had these sky-high visions and lofty goals (best-selling author! president! movie star! writer at HBO!), but maybe I should just come down to earth and be at peace with someone special, but that has also proven problematic. I just never thought that I was "enough" for anyone, even for myself. And then I held every man to a higher standard, and none of them measured up either. My situation kept me feeling that I could never have the man of my dreams because he would want to be with someone who was richer, smarter, thinner, prettier. And then the cancer came along, and I became even more of an outcast. Who wants to be with that?

Let's face it. Women do low-class, after-hours work most often because their day job sucks or doesn't exist. And that is a political problem more than an ambition problem. Or maybe it's just priorities. Then, everything from decent real estate to decent healthcare to decent education is priced for people who make at least six figures, but that is only about 10% of the population. Without googling it, my guess is this group is mostly male and mostly white. You know, the most ambitious, hardest working group in America. The rest of us flounder around trying to cobble together an existence that hovers just slightly above subsistence. Oh, dear, does that sound like a whiny little bitch? Oh, well.

So I gave up the night gigs when I tried to be a teacher and a wife. But neither of those roles was right for me, either. And there was still the frustration of not quite being financially independent, which can wear on a person, especially when they feel like they did all the requisite work to get there.

So anyway...

I started the hormone treatment again, and who knows how long I will have to be on it this time and what if it doesn't work? And then I might have to do chemo again, and what if the chemo doesn't work, and then I have to have surgery again and the stuff just keeps coming back??! It becomes just another chore after a while. Like cleaning the bathtub once a year.

When I was young, I had estrogen but no money, so I couldn't have a relationship. Now I have money, but no estrogen, so I still can't have a relationship. And that's probably all I really want. Maybe. No, it's not all I want. The question is not, *What do you want?* It's, *What can you not live without?* What do you want the *most?* No matter what you want, you face the immediate realization that you probably won't be able to get it. Attaining a degree of contentment is a matter of wanting what you already have, placing a value on that, and then crafting goals that *are* attainable. But how do you figure out what's attainable and what's not? Perhaps something along the lines of giving up on delusional sky-high goals, but where's the fun in that?

I know other people have been through worse, but that doesn't make it any easier, that kind of thinking. Like, *Whew! Thank goodness, somebody else is more fucked up than I am!* How is that a positive? It just means there's even more suffering than I can ever imagine in the world. That's even more depressing.

What I say to my shrinks: "I am recovering from cancer, I have no job, no husband, no children, my father is passed, my mother has Alzheimer's, my brothers don't ever ask how I am and they live five minutes away. I live in the outskirts of a village, and I am struggling to find one or two people I can talk to or be with."

I know I am not alone.

Or am I?

BUT I do have a lovely little cabin in the woods and my bills are paid. I can just be here and enjoy this place I have worked very hard on for a number of years. I am lucky to still be alive to enjoy it. And to be able to help my mother. And there it is: Simple goals that I have already reached. For a moment, I can feel successful. (Deep inhale, exhale)

(Giving myself a moment)

But what does one do to escape the isolation?

Take road trips!!

Road Trip Diary 2015:

Left Michigan Jan 21st.

Iowa: one night at aunt and uncle's

Nebraska: Hampton Inn one night

Colorado: cousin two nights

Richfield, Utah: Hampton Inn one night. HBO!

Vegas: at a friend's empty condo 6 days and nights. Saw friends, hiked Red Rock, and made use of the spa at Bellagio! Also saw the show Jubilee *just to see cheesy traditional Vegas in person and check out the competition ;) And the costuming!*

California: dinner with my old photographer friend in Burbank.

Santa Barbara: one night

Cambria, CA: at the Fog Catcher for two days and nights. This place is along Moonstone Beach. Right before San Simeon. I have little interest in Mr. Hearst's castle, however, and the tour takes two hours.

Drove to Sonora through endless vineyards, green ranches, and dry farmland, to visit family for three rainy days.

Drove through rainy Monterey to rainy Morro Bay that night and camped (cramped) out by the bay. ("Cramping": my term for sleeping in the car)

Let's take a moment to deconstruct "camping."

You drive 1000 miles, walk all day long, and then get somewhere and think, *Fuck, where am I? And I don't have Wi-Fi or anything else, and now I have to fucking sleep here?* What is the point of being in a beautiful place if you're going to be asleep? You may think it's so great. *I'm going to sleep under the stars.* But your body is saying:

What the fuck?

Where are we sleeping?

What are we sleeping on?

How dare you make me sleep on—what is this?

A fucking yoga mat?

It's like an inch thick.

I can feel the ground.

Motherfucker.

You think this is acceptable to me?

No, this is not an appropriate place for this body to be sleeping, OK?

Fuck you and your stars.

The human race has evolved to this amazing point where we know how to build whole houses made of brick and steel and wood and insulation and drywall and all kinds of stuff with an actual solid *roof* on it.

But no! You're gonna leave all that and go backwards in time and try to live like some indigenous cultures did 1000 fucking years ago, sleeping on the filthy ground with some sort of ridiculous flimsy tarp over your head, with *no* bathroom!!

You have to light a fire to cook anything and no fucking electricity and forget Wi-Fi.

What are you, homeless?

Fuck this.

So the answer is RVing. Yes, that's right, drag your entire house with you across the goddamn country using insane amounts of fuel, and then you have to find a space to rent, dump your shit, hook up to power and water with a bunch of other freaking mobile living rooms surrounding you.

Might as well be living in an apartment building. Only it's *so great!* You can *move* it! And pay more money to do that and pay more money again at the next stop.

Ah, yes, this is freedom.

(Back to the trip)

Sun came back out the next morning.

(Discovered that you have to put quarters into the shower in any California state park.)

Drove south on PCH, stopped at beautiful bluffs off 101 in Carpinteria.

Then to Two Bunch Palms Spa in Desert Hot Springs. Mud bath and arnica body wrap. *Absolutely essential.*

After Desert Hot Springs, it was time to start meandering back to Michigan, via Vegas. Google told me the shortest route to Vegas from where I was in California was through the Mohave National Preserve. Little did I know that road has not been well preserved. Every hundred feet it was *kerchunk kerchunk*. And it was nighttime with no lights at all for miles. No gas, no phone service. I was so happy to finally see the lights from a casino emerge in the distance. That was my only questionable choice the whole trip. Honest.

Stayed four days in Vegas again, but at a cheap hotel, just to get one more taste of Red Rock, yoga, Pilates, and a Gershwin concert. Yes, there is "culture" in Vegas.

Dropped down to Arches National Park where I got pics of the "three gossips" when the sun came out just before noon.

Stunning drive with clear blue sky from Moab to see friends in Questa, NM. Near Taos. Truly therapeutic.

Never settle!!

7 wobbly concepts embodied by single words:

"Happy"

What exactly does this mean? Does it mean excited? Does it mean content? Are we happy if we are only happy for two minutes or two hours? Is it possible to be ceaselessly happy for an entire year? A day? Can happiness make you cry? Can we be happy without being sad sometimes? Is this supposed to be our goal in life? Rather elusive, isn't it? I will just lie and tell everyone that I am happy all the time, and then they will all be jealous of me forever. Because happiness is knowing you can make others jealous.

"Deserve"

People who are born rich deserve to be born rich. People who are born in the ghetto deserve to be born in the ghetto. No, of course not. That would not make sense. It's pure chance and circumstance. But you have to admit, one of these is the better choice. This is a major problem in American society: the worship of wealth and of those who have it. There may be evidence that society respects the self-made wealth over the inherited wealth, but still, by and large, if we know certain people just have more wealth than we do, regardless of whence it came, we feel like we need to make some sort of internal pagan sacrifice at the altar of the wealth of this other. And because everyone wants to be worshipped, everyone is willing to do all manner of ill if they think it will lead to this form of idolatry. Circumstances determine choices.

"Fault"

We waste monumental amounts of energy deciding who is at fault for anything, large or small, societal, political, economic, or personal. Ultimately, nothing is ever completely one person's fault. There is always some circumstance that contributes to the unfortunate event. If the boy had not been so angry at his mother for locking him in the closet for a week, he would not have stabbed her. If people were not forced to buy a car to get to work, there wouldn't be climate change. If society did not place such huge pressure on us to get as much money as possible by any means possible, people would not resort to money laundering and embezzlement. There may be people out there who think they are above such social influence, but they were probably born into relatively decent circumstances. Circumstances can change. And not always for the better.

"Family"

We are thrown into this world with a group of people we had no hand in choosing. *Someone else* decided that we would be born, and when. And yet we are made to feel responsible for everything that happens to us after our happenstance birth. We did not have any chance for preparation or planning. We are made to feel beholden to and obligated to this particular group of people, no matter how we are treated by them. Why? Are blood relations somehow sacred? To be trusted automatically? So many people have been abandoned, abused, or neglected by those who brought them into this world and those related to them. And they *trusted* them.

"Trust"

Another slippery concept. Trust is a delicate, highly prized trinket that is never quite fully earned or paid off. Maybe you can trust someone today, but not tomorrow. And how far can you trust someone? Can you trust that this person would not stick a fork in you at 16,000 feet when stranded on a mountain for weeks? Some people will never trust anyone ever, and for good reason. If a person has never had anyone in their life whom they felt they could trust, or if their trust was betrayed in a brutal way at a vulnerable point, then no, they should not be expected to trust anyone ever again.

"Respect"

This relies completely on your audience. Respect from whom? And why? And do you respect your audience enough to care about earning their respect?

"*Love*"

Don't make me laugh. This word is pure fantasy and means something different to every single individual on the planet. Plus the meaning changes based on the context and the user. Therefore, it is useless.

The Men All Pause

What happens at menopause is that the fog clears. The woman is no longer enveloped in a hormonally driven delirium. There is no man who appeals to her anymore because she can see clearly now; the estrogen is gone. And men can tell when a woman is post-menopausal because she just stares right through them to their core and isn't afraid to say exactly what she sees there —not only to him but to anybody else she feels like talking to.

She doesn't care anymore. And that's what makes her finally free.

Free at last.

Free at last.

Some people complain that surrogacy is pregnancy with a profit motive. But a lot of women get married at least partly due to a profit motive. It can be called financial security motive, but that's just semantics. Is this not also exploitation? Does surrogacy exploit women's bodies in a different way than any pregnancy does? We can have cattle farms and fish farms, but it's not okay to breed humans? I thought human farms were the suburbs. Isn't that what we have been doing since the beginning of time? Men have always viewed marriage and reproduction partly as a commercial transaction and business opportunity for future profit generation. Parents assume that their kids will generate income, which could eventually help them in old age. Do you think they would want to have kids if they thought those kids would never make any money?

I just hope that all people stop thinking that the Marriage, Kids, and Mortgage holy trinity is the aim of life. It's like saying the default state of being is misery. Because all three of those things *will* cause *some* degree of misery. They *might* cause some degree of satisfaction. Call me a cynic, but that's what the stats show. It would be nice if everyone could find work they love that paid over six figures, a mate who was always loving and faithful, and had kids who were eternal angels.

Parents try to make childfree people feel guilty, like they have no purpose in life without kids. But what they are really saying is, "What gives you the right not to be miserable and overburdened like everybody else?" As if people without kids should feel bad about having fewer burdens, because they have no *right* and no *reason* to feel happy without kids. If a parent was truly happy to be a parent, he or she would feel no need to criticize non-parents.

When you go through this horrifying process called menopause, you get to this realization that your entire life has really been driven by hormones because now that you no longer have them, you see no point in doing anything anymore. No longer are these evil chemicals coursing through your veins making you do things that you would rather not remember—and probably can't. But suddenly…suddenly you can think clearly for the first time in your life.

And it sucks.

You are no longer at the mercy of the whims of whatever man you happen to be attracted to. There is no intimidation anymore. You look at the opposite sex and think: "What did I ever see in *that*?"

"I was influenced by *that*?"

"I was in love with *that*?"

"I was stressed out over *that*?"

And it just blows my mind how much time, energy, and money I wasted struggling to be attractive or pining away over some man or another.

Why does menopause start with "men"? It should be womenopause. Too many syllables, I guess. Just say womenpause then. Or menpause. Because it does happen on both sides of the equation.

Vagipause (for lube)

penipause (for Viagra)

Why does menstruation start with "men"?

Why does mental start with "men"?

What about ménage à trois?

*man*ufacture

*man*ipulation

*man*euver

Well, the English language has been *man*-handled after all.

The great thing about being over 50 is that you are now living in the future you were so worried about when you were younger. You know you're getting old when you start wondering if you will expire before your credit cards. But it's fine. You can live for the moment and just be a teenager every fucking day because this is it—this is all you get. You don't have a future to worry about anymore. The other great thing is that the stress about pissing anybody off and losing a job/house is over. Financial independence, even at a low level of subsistence, is a great thing.

Today I found out that I can get a tumor fried off my liver even though they have to shut off my right lung during the procedure to do it. Then I had a conversation with my 84-year-old temporary roommate in Ann Arbor, and she said I still haven't learned anything from writing my first book because I'm still looking for someone else to make me happy. And then my financial advisor told me that $10,000 is a big chunk to take out all at once, so we should talk.

Letter to my oncologist:

Sept. 2015

As you may recall, I had a total abdominal hysterectomy and 6 rounds of Taxol in 2003. Then I had a good 10 years cancer free. Then came 2013. I saw you for a second opinion in August 2013 after this second recurrence of granulosa cell ovarian cancer.

I got 9 rounds of Abraxane, thinking I was going to get good results with that since the Taxol appeared to get me 10 years. But my blood marker never came down far enough.

After the chemo was done and I came back to Michigan, the marker was still sort of high, so I went to Cancer Treatment Center of America (expensive) and to you for second opinions, and hormone therapy was held out as the solution. I started receiving the shots once a month. In the ass!

So I had 9 months of Lupron from August 2013 to April 2014. And it worked! I also got a clear CT scan in April.

It did work. For a while. I had to go back on Lupron for six months, then got my time off for good behavior starting in May 2015. I got another CT scan in August, and it showed a couple of 2cm implants on the right liver lobe. Got another Lupron shot three days later.

Yes. This has been quite a ride.

So anyway, my other doc swears that the Lupron will shrink the two implants and that it should make a difference by December, so I am going to get another CT at end of Nov.

You are the 9th doctor I have seen for this problem that started in 1996 with the right ovary rupturing on a beautiful day in June.

I have read that liver metastasis with this particular cancer is extremely rare, and this is a small recurrence, right? Not a whole bunch of tumors like last time. Right?

What are the chances that I can ever get rid of this stuff for good and go on to die in a fiery plane crash in the Sierra Nevada mountains at the age of 93?

Hey, it's my dream.

And thank you for saving lives.

Hopefully mine too.

Cancer is kind of a series of battles and skirmishes and truces and treaties. It's advances and concessions. It's trade-offs. No one ever really wins, because if the cancer wins, it dies too, because it had a home in your body, which is no longer available.

My 84-year-old girlfriend was sound asleep as I tiptoed down the stairs and out the door at 4:45 a.m. I had not slept much that night and had actually taken a shower at 2 a.m. The taxi pulled up right on schedule in front of the trellis that marked the path to the little house hidden on the corner in Ann Arbor. I ran over the pavers and under the trellis and hopped into the van from the Amazing Blue taxi company. A young man from Pakistan was the driver. He had just graduated a year ago from Michigan State, and was planning on going to medical school. We had a conversation about the weather, cancer, and the pros and cons of vegetarian diets, as he drove me to the University Hospital.

I was slated for radiofrequency ablation for the small tumor on the back of my liver. You've never heard of that? It's basically having a needle stuck into your side that somehow winds its way to the tumor site under the guidance of ultrasound imaging. Oh, yes, an actual person has to stick the needle in, I think. Videotaping every medical procedure would be so enlightening for the patient. I would like some proof that they actually did what they said they did. Aren't I just turning my unconscious body over to the medical community and trusting that they will do that thing we discussed? That thing I signed off on? There is no greater vulnerability. So much trust is needed. A person can break your heart, but medical people can break your life.

The young man dropped me off in front of the main hospital, and the place was deserted. There was a woman at the desk outside the building, and I asked her how to find the right floor. That building is a labyrinth.

So then starts the long waiting period. They want you there at 6 a.m. for check-in, and then they walk you to pre-op and put you behind a

curtain and tell you to change into that ridiculous gown and then....
And then. You lie there for almost 2 hours and various nurses come
in and ask you the same damn questions. Then the anesthesiologist
comes in and asks you more damn questions that are pretty much
along the same lines.

When was the last time you ate?

Do you wear contacts?

Do you have loose teeth?

Do you wear dentures?

Are you diabetic?

Are you allergic to any medications?

And of course,

What's your date of birth?

What's your date of birth?

What's your date of birth?

No one had shown so much interest in me in years.

So. After surviving cancer by the removal of all problematic organs,
the injection of poison in my veins, shots of a drug that put me in
menopause times ten, and having a nodule fried off my liver, what do
I do now? And who is going to want me now? What do I fix first? My

emotional self, my sexual self, my spiritual self, or my financial self? Do I fix my vagina, my thighs, my face, or my brain first? Face and vagina same time. Then mix in thighs. And then the brain, pulling up the rear. As if my brain has the ability to do that.

I don't know about you, but I cannot think straight until after midnight. This is about the time that I have worked through all the superficial bullshit in my brain and can finally get back to trying to figure out the meaning of my life and I actually do figure out approximately 1% of that meaning between the hours of midnight and 4 a.m. My only problem is, by the time I wake up I can't remember what that 1% was or if it even matters anymore because the meaning changes overnight. I am cursed with this obsession of always trying to find *meaning* in everything that happens to me. Nothing in my life can be meaning-*less*; it must be meaning*ful*. And I will inspect something and analyze something for ever and ever and ever to find some meaning in it. To the point of insanity. Because as much as I don't want to even entertain the possibility, it is very possible that most things, in fact, don't *mean* a damn thing.

So what is the meaning of all this?

PART IV
This Is Real...and Surreal

The conundrum in later life is figuring out if you are really ready to forget about making any more money. No one is ever ready. Either you still need more money for basic needs or you still need more money for your basic ego. Because this is America and that's what we do here. Once you stop making money, there is nothing to do but watch the next generation take over and watch your own self decay. It's truly astounding how much of our identity is derived from our financial standing or our looks or lack thereof. Oh sure, you can go to the gym, take online classes, and have cosmetic work done, but there is no getting around the fact that your life is more than half over and you don't have the same options you had at 21.

You might, however, have new options that you did not have earlier. The only way to stay optimistic is to believe that the second half of life will be better than the first—primarily because you finally do have *some* money and maybe a bit of wisdom, wisdom being the more important of the two. But then you have to ask yourself: Is youth plus poverty better than age plus money? Keep in mind that youth carries with it the possibility of getting out of poverty.

Speaking of money, do you ever wish you were Mark Zuckerberg? Or Jeff Bezos? It would be nice to go shopping for an island. Time to realize, although too late, that there is not much value in voluntary poverty, which was what I thought I had signed on for by majoring in dance. But there is also no fulfillment in doing work you hate just for the money. There is no satisfaction in pursuing a particular path only because it *might* lead to money. There is no happiness derived from spending money, only a fleeting feel-good minute or two.

So what is a person to do? If you don't create things that are popular, you will not have an audience for the things that you create. But if you play to the crowds, you will probably just create crap. Is Facebook crap? Is Twitter crap? They make money. Is money crap? It depends. Is there substance in the content generated? Sometimes. Except in my case, of course. My content is always stellar.

Money is crap if it just turns into more crap. And that is why I am in the strip club taking advantage of the wealth redistribution that comes from men throwing away discretionary income on something as useless and fleeting as a lap dance. I can take the money they are wasting and turn it into something beautiful and useful, like my cabin or this book you are reading. (Insert happy face emoji)

I am starting to think that most of my problems stem from the fact that somewhere along the way I was made to think that the world's problems were somehow my responsibility; that I am supposed to "make the world a better place."

Let's deconstruct that:

First of all, how are the world's problems my problems? Did I cause these problems? No. So why is it even any of my business what these problems are? I would rather be in blissful ignorance as I am a sensitive person and can barely deal with my own existential crises.

And even if I did think I should do something about said problems, why should I think that I am so omniscient that I have any fucking ability to have any impact whatsoever on said problems? Honestly, even US Presidents have not had that much impact in the greater scheme of things:

We still have war.

We still have disease.

We still have poverty.

We still have environmental degradation.

We still have masses of ignorant people.

We still have gross economic inequality.

We still have racism, sexism, classism.

And we still have Donald Trump, who overtly believes that since he has more money than most people, he therefore has all the answers, is inherently "better" than everyone else, and has the right to lie indiscriminately. It's like that song from Fiddler on the Roof: *Cause when*

you're rich, they think you really know. But in his case, we only think
we know he's rich.

Isn't that the real issue that no one wants to address? Are billionaires
"better" than the rest of us? Even if they inherited everything, doesn't
the better lifestyle and access to the best of everything make the person "better"? Do people really think that *character* and dealing with
adversity make a person "better," or is it just access to the high-end
people, schools, and overall lifestyle that automatically makes a person
high-end? Or does it just create a narcissistic bloviator? What exactly
is a high-quality person? Is there any consensus on this question? The
rich may actually believe that they are rich enough to dispense with
any sort of moral compass. Like morals are just for the classes beneath
them, to keep them there. 45 billion dollars? Can any *one* person be
trusted to have that much money and not become a corrupt individual? I guess that's the whole basis for "progressive" tax reform. This is
a capitalist game, and the way to win is to take everybody's stuff. For
very cheap. Then sell it for way more.

Perhaps I can generalize here and propose the following core differen-
tiation between conservatives and liberals. Conservatives draw a hard
line: it's either good or bad, poor or rich, hot or cold. Only things that
can be measured down to the thread matter. If it can't be measured, it
can't matter. So they measure income. And thread counts. Liberals are
more nuanced in their analysis of people and events. They are less likely
to judge and dismiss those who appear at first glance to not measure
up according to conventional standards. They question the standards
and the measuring stick itself. I have to prove to the world that even
though I don't make a ton of dough, I can still make bread unlike any

other. I just have to entice people to eat it. *Come on! It's good for you. Only a little bit seedy.*

Anyway, 45 Presidents and all the above-mentioned problems are still there at varying levels, depending on who is measuring them. If only everyone lived like I do, we wouldn't have these problems at all.

My Executive Order—Everyone must replicate my lifestyle:

- Renovate and live in an old cabin in a rural area.
- Don't have kids.
- If you drive, drive a hybrid or electric car.
- Only buy one computer every 10 years.
- Only buy one car every 20 years.
- Think Read Teach Dance.
- Be active and an activist.
- Eat organic food.
- And don't work for any company that treats people or the planet like cannon fodder.

Don't tell me I never gave you anything. This is good advice. The only problem is, no one will follow it.

My real problem, though (so many of them), is that I have this damn need for integrity. Everything I say, think, do, own, and exude must be aligned with my own personal value system. I am incapable of doing a job that does not reflect that system. And I do not believe in anything that contains even a whiff of the mundane or the vacuous. It has to have attitude, creativity, depth, and a mission. And not require a bunch of tech skills. My search will go on…

And I know you are thinking: Oh, wait, didn't you work in a strip club? How exactly does that square with your precious personal values?

That is an excellent question! But I believe I did address this earlier: To execute the proper reinvestment of wealth redistribution. And to uphold my personal value of eating.

Self-doubt is the reason so many women fail to reach their full potential. Aren't we supposed to aim high and reach for the stars like everyone else? Yet every time I did, someone complained that I was always trying to take over the world, and if I need to perform, why the hell can't I just be content with singing in the church choir? Why do you have to go audition for *The Voice*? Of all the outlandish things. Who do you think you are? Rihanna? Just be the boring run-of-the-mill middle-aged Midwestern woman that you are and learn to love it.

Siblings are the reason why people want their own family. Or they are the reason not to have a family at all. I guess I feel like I don't have my own "team" of built-in cheerleaders, yet how many children are supportive of things their parents are doing? I guess by the time you're the age of a parent, you are not supposed to need support anymore. And let's face it, how many people are truly supportive of anyone? And if *I don't believe in myself*, it doesn't matter what anyone else thinks. And *if I do believe in myself*, it doesn't matter what anyone else thinks. But sometimes it's nice just to have *one* person in your cheering section. I have to think of past success—even if it means going all the way back to high school or college. Whatever it takes. If you are not going to aim high, you might as well stay in bed. And eat crackers. Which is what I have been doing for the last three days.

Speaking of aiming high, I have to keep working in the club at least awhile longer. I mean, I just bought two new bras. I keep asking my friends if they will help me get some job when I'm too old to do that crap anymore, but I may be almost 60 by the time that happens. So I get to go straight from sexism to ageism, and that bridge is the shortest bridge in America for women.

Why do women want to be sexy when we know that sexy might lead to sex, which leads to falling in love, pregnancy, or STDs? Or even (gasp) *marriage?* First we are trained to be sexy, and then we are conditioned to remain sexy. *Forever.* Even growing old*er* is not allowed. But like I said, I don't have to worry about that shit anymore because the men have all paused. Actually, they have stopped. Should be Men All Stop. What no one tells you is that this Post-Menopausal World is the land of the free and the home of the brave. "Free at last! Free at last! Thank God almighty, I am free of that!"

I looked into this full-time employment deal and realized it really wasn't my thing. Full-time employment, a mortgage for a POS house, and *having kids*—holy shit, why torture yourself? And them? These are just conventional forms of masochism, and I can accomplish that in so many other more creative ways.

SEX is overrated. Having a house you can't pay cash for is overrated. Having kids is overrated. Being employed—unless for yourself—is WAY overrated, no matter how much you get paid. If you are working for someone else, chances are you hate what you do, and you hate your boss. Come on, be honest with yourself. The concept of the "work ethic" was created by slave owners. Rich white men. There are people in this world who have never worked a regular job for a day in their lives and they are *BILLIONAIRES*!! It takes more than working a regular job to become a billionaire. You're not gonna become a billionaire driving a fucking Uber. It takes around half a billion, plus time, and a few decent investment choices, and you can hire a guy to make those choices for you. That's pretty much it. No real "work" involved.

Sometimes I drive through so-called normal neighborhoods in Midwestern towns, and I look at the houses and think of how I never lived in one of those.

I lived

on a farm

in a cabin

in a loft

or in a condo

my whole life.

What if I gave up too much?

What if I sacrificed things that I shouldn't have sacrificed?

Or did I ever really have a choice?

Law school and medical school both seemed beyond me and beneath me, if that's possible.

What if all this pursuit of things that I couldn't even envision just wasn't worth it?

I'm supposed to have something to *show* for all of my efforts, right? Yet they say failure is the pathway to success.

How much failure can I sustain?

How much failure do I have *time* for?

What did I get in place of the things that I *might've* had if I had taken another route?

What if I am just a person sitting down and documenting her inner chaos and shortcomings with brutal honesty? As if that will somehow wind up being a positive thing? Am I even doing that very well?

It always keeps changing: my idea of who I think I am or who I think I could or should be. Do I think I would have been better at being a wife and mother? In a word: NO. That was not a sacrifice; it was a choice that served my chosen lifestyle, the style of insane improvisation. For someone with that lifestyle, having kids would be cruel.

I am going to be totally politically incorrect here and say that *perhaps* the whole habit of reproduction is somewhat delusional and selfish. No, I'm going to be motherfucking *real* and say it *is* delusional and selfish.

Think about it.

People literally do that to themselves *on purpose*, knowing full well the consequences of their actions. I mean, look at that— you just created more human suffering. That thing *came in crying*, did it not?!

SOA. Suffering On Arrival.

Then we cry upon departure too.

And there's even more suffering at that point for others.

Not making judgments, just stating facts. I could be wrong.

What if the unborn could see everything that's happening in the world and they knew all the history of the world and they could decide when, how, where, why, and to whom they want to be born?

What choices would they make?

Yeah, yeah, I look like someone who might have been a cheerleader at one point or another in her life and my first name is spelled like the merry in Merry Christmas. Fun! Happy! Oh gosh what a perfect name for a cheerleader.

Yeah, I was a cheerleader.

But you know what happens after you're really optimistic and play a *motivational* role by being the "go team go" person when you're young? You become the exact inverse of that as an older lady in direct proportion to the degree you were that cheerful. You become the most bitter sarcastic crass ornery rude bitch in the world. It's "go team go" to "fuck you motherfuckers."

You know, I'm just going to get a boob job when I'm 60, and then my career is really going to take off. I am not gonna be some flash in the pan. No, I want to go from the frying pan to the fire. Because I'm a really good cook.

It's just slightly past middle-age when we finally realize we wasted a lot of time thinking we had to please anybody but ourselves and thinking that we somehow had to be *responsible* for something or someone.

No, there isn't a whole lot that any ONE person is responsible for in this world.

Just:

take care of yourself

pay your bills

don't kill anybody

recycle

That's about it.

Even stealing is kind of a gray area. I mean how easy is it for a pair of socks just to waft their way inside of a towel, and then you go to self-checkout and forget that the socks are there?

Go to Walmart at 2 a.m. and use their self-checkout. It's easy as fuck to forget stuff then.

You might be thinking that I am a judgmental person by now. And you are probably laying judgments on me as a person too. It happens. I don't judge judgments. But think of the judgments we lay on certain jobs:

bus boy

janitor

maid

stripper

Uber driver

taxi driver

dry cleaner

garbage man or woman

truck driver

waitress/waiter

bartender

K-12 teacher

Basically, anybody who's not a doctor or lawyer or a CEO is just shit apparently, including teachers.

Are lawyers "better" than teachers?

Is a minister "better" than a used car salesman? Even if the used car salesman makes way more money?

Is a Wall Street trader a worse person than a doctor? Or just lower status regardless of income? Is a mechanic higher status than a truck-driver? Is a stripper lower status than a hair stylist?

The judgment is real.

Why am I trying to get back into the entertainment industry?

Because I still give good headshot.

LOL!

Let's face it. They don't give out awards to cancer survivors. They don't pay you for struggling. You don't win the Nobel Peace prize for surviving a miserable childhood. The struggle is real.

Nobody gives a shit, but you keep thinking:

oh

all this hardship

it's creating such an amazing character in me

it's making me better

whatever doesn't kill me makes me stronger

blah blah blah blah

Ever since I had the cancer and got through the cancer and recovered from the cancer, I've been tricking my brain into thinking I'm still the same person that I was, and I guess if I can just maintain that delusion I can somehow feel like I'm still me.

I'm still strong

I'm still sexy

still smart

and above all

confident.

I can still take on the world even if none of those things are objectively true. If I can just somehow maintain that delusion, then I can

keep getting out of bed

keep making plans

and keep trying.

Speaking of trying:

Watching CNN is like watching your house burn down while being
completely powerless to do anything about it.

And doing that every fucking night.

That's not healthy.

It's basically torture.

It's masochism.

It's like cutting yourself,

giving yourself a cigarette burn every night.

(SIGH)

I'll take $1 billion over "character" any day.

We are gathered here today to mourn the death of M. B. Clark.

She is survived by her credit cards.

I see out in the pews,

we have here the representatives of

Discover

American Express

Citibank

Capital One

Bank of America

Barclay Bank

all the revolving doors of debt.

Please don't let the door hit you on the way out.

Long live her debt.

But anyway, I'm not going to waste time crying just because I'm not young anymore, because that will just use up the time that I have left to make the most of just being alive.

So choosing not to be married, not to have children, and not to have a regular job unless backed into a corner amounts to choosing to be unAmerican. *What? You aren't going to take part in the dog-eat-dog world and claw your way to mediocrity by spending half your income on rent and all of your energy spinning your wheels and bludgeoning your head against a brick wall? You're not going to partake in the mass masochism of reproduction?*

Um. No.

MY LIFE IN CLASSIC ROCK SONG TITLES:

I was going for Big Love and the Big Time when I came across a Magic Bus and I knew I needed a little Foreplay.

"You Wreck Me," he told me.

"Who Do You Love? Who Are You? I Won't Get Fooled Again," I stated.

"That's What I Like About You," he replied with a wink.

So I took a Walk on the Wild Side with him and found myself On the Dark Side and was Thunderstruck at the Witchy Woman I had become. I needed One Bourbon, One Scotch and for sure a Beer.

I wondered aloud, "When Will I Be Loved?"

"Get Over It," he ordered. "We are Born to Run and Born to Be Wild."

"I Will Survive!" I roared at him.

Shattered, I Ran.

I talked to my Old Man, and asked him to look at my life.

He just told me I was Blowin' in the Wind.

Sort of Like a Rolling Stone.

Again, I Ran Over the Hills and Far Away, past the Misty Mountain Hop, back to the Hotel California.

And it was all More Than A Feeling.

For What it's Worth.

There was a Brick House and a Cabin Down Below, but I was looking for Wildflowers.

Stayin' Alive was all I was tryin' to do, and so I Worked Hard for the Money, while they Played That Funky Music.

Money Talks, right?

"Call Me."

As for those auditions for *The Voice* in Chicago, I was unprepared to face one teenage boy sitting at a folding table staring at his laptop with a "Magic Bus" sticker on the back of it. It was a small conference room set up with chairs in a circle like a support group. Each of us went up to the middle of the circle to the tape on the floor. The mark was placed so that we could not see anyone behind us and those behind us could only see our backside. What? No microphone? No stage? Only one "judge"? And he certainly did not have his back turned. So I guess looks count, per usual.

I sang "They Can't Take That Away from Me" to this boy who could have been my nephew. They sure can. Yes, indeed, they can take that away from me. But I will go back again. Sing something Sinatra. Or maybe "Alfie." Something the kids have never heard. I must expand their cultural horizons. The future depends on it.

(My computer does not trust me. It always asks me if I am *sure* I want to delete something. Yes, I'm sure! Stop doubting my judgment, you fucking smart machine. I don't need any more reminders that you are smarter than me!)

Dating in my twenties was like a buffet, a smorgasbord of fresh and lively choices in sizes, flavors, shapes, and colors. There was novelty and variety, new models always coming out. Now, it's leftovers, day-old bread, recycled and second-hand crap, damaged goods, recalls, and scratch-and-dent floor models. I may be a little dented here and there myself, but not to the degree where I am unrecognizable when compared to my 25-year-old self. At least that's what I like to keep telling myself.

The songs I sing in the shower have also changed over the years. In my 20s, I hummed, "Getting to know you. Getting to know all about you." Yesterday I found myself singing, "I'm so glad we had this time together, just to share a laugh and sing a song." Yes, it seemed I did just get started, and now the time has come to say...where are those Wheat Thins? Funny they are called Wheat Thins instead of Wheat Fats. Because that's what they do.

Questions as an aging gypsy/cancer survivor:

Should I assume that I have beaten the cancer, even if I still have to get further treatment? (It's not going to kill me, but it might throw a few more punches.)

If I need more treatment, will that keep me from being fully physical and sexual? Will it keep me from having a sex/love life?

Do I stick it out in the sticks of Michigan for a longer haul because my mom is here, my doc is here, and my cabin is here? I even have a few friends here.

Do I take another chance on the California dream?

Or do I just travel out there in the winter and make the best of that?

And what exactly does the phrase "the future" mean? It's a rather nebulous and relative term, isn't it?

Or do I just move to NYC on my own without much of a plan, but enough money to get started? Like I went to LA in 1995.

Well, we saw how that turned out.

LETTERS (some fake, some not):

Dear Manager of Strip Club:

Just a "heads" up, and a plan for a just in case:

There is a possibility that I will have to go through chemo again this winter.

If this is so, here is my idea for turning a negative into a positive:

I would like to dance bald in a packed club and have someone film it. This would help me promote my book Stripping Down to the Bones *as that is exactly what I would be doing: even the head has no clothes.*

I would start out with a wig, and then rip that off too.

I just wanted to check on this a "head" of time and make sure it would be okay with you. It could also be promoted as another kind of freak show. (Bald stripper vs. sword swallower)

Of course, I would have to wait for the chemo to be over and the white blood cell count to be up before I could come back into that germy place.

Great way to kick off the season!

So let's be creative. I'm game.

Letter to Women's Studies professors:

I have trodden places that most self-respecting college-educated white women would never dare. I was in situations that I knew would not look good on a resume. And some of this was on purpose, out of a desire to see life and American society from all perspectives, not from an ivory tower or safe haven. How else to get to the bare bones of the truth about American culture except by way of the underground?

How did I keep my wits about me? Maybe I didn't. How did I have the courage to write about this experience, knowing that it may not reflect well on me as a professional person? But to me, "professional" refers not to what a person does, but to how and why.

Please find enclosed a book that I began in 1996 and finished while going through chemo in Las Vegas in 2013. Hey, Rome wasn't built in a day. I am working on two other books, but I cannot forecast whether I will live long enough to complete anything else beyond what I already have.

The title is both literal and metaphorical. Regarding the literal part, I went into the strip club environment with the eye and ear of a journalist, as a researcher of sorts. I always treated each chapter of my life as a research or creative project, especially when I was intersecting with the sex industry. It is highly improbable that anyone who has not been intimately involved with this industry can write about it with any authority. Taking off one's clothes in the presence of strangers means becoming as vulnerable as one possibly can be, both in body and mind, yet it can be ultimately empowering. How can power be derived from vulnerability?

As for the metaphor, I went about drilling down through the layers of American society and getting down to the bares bones of my own identity, simultaneously. Going through chemo also forces a woman to question who she is beyond her looks and sexuality. There are few experiences more "bare bones" than being a bald woman. The bones also refers to the ashes of my father and what is still left there, with him, to be unearthed.

Was I a sex worker? What exactly is that? And why are "sex workers" lumped in a category called "marginalized populations"? Is the American sex industry good, bad, or neutral? How can women be strong in it rather than weak? What is the overall long-term effect it has on women who work in it? What happens to them after they get out of it? How many never get out? Do they like it? Hate it? Why?

These are the questions I am still trying to answer using my own personal experience. Because I may still work in a strip club not because I need to, but because I am keeping an eye on the girls. And on the boys. And taking notes.

The following is a short list of all the themes the book touches on:

Being an Underdog

Rural America

Organic Farming

The 80s and 90s

Family

Dance

University of Michigan

Cancer

9-11

Ambition

Cults

Strip clubs

Marriage

Divorce

Vegas

Hollywood

Education

Economy

America as a concept

Sex

Gender

Politics

Rape

Women

Men

Media

Religion

Love

Beauty

Resilience

Alienation

Too much?

Sometimes that scene from *Titanic* plays in my head, the one after the ship has struck the berg and is obviously fatally wounded. The powers that be all gather in the captain's quarters, and they roll out the blueprint of the ship. While Mr. Andrews is assessing the damage, the pushy Mr. Ismay demands, "When can we get underway, dammit?" He is met with the answer that it is a mathematical certainty the *Titanic* will sink.

"This ship can't sink," gasps Ismay.

"She's made of iron, sir. I assure you she can. And she will...,"
returns Andrews.

M. B. can't die!

"She's made of carbon, my friend. I assure you she can."

"How much time?" she asks the doctor. "What about hormone
therapy?"

"That buys you months only."

"Exercise? The right diet?"

Silence.

Sleep eludes at night.

Wonder what I can eat.

Have to kill this fly.

My zebra-striped bathrobe keeps me company.

It's approaching 3 a.m.

I am considering walking back
across the yard
to my mother's house
to check on her
and watch HBO.

Have you ever spent all day just looking at calendars? How can I plan until after the scan?

Live for today. Okay, what about next week? How do I know what to do today if I don't even know what I'll be able to do next week?

And then there is the old flame from junior high school...you know, the knight in shining armor who takes 30 years to resurface, but he is only separated, and you are just old. And nowhere near as rich as he is.

So there are now three things that turn me into an exile, as I am part of three distinct marginalized populations: dancers, cancer survivors, and single women in rural America.

Nobody wants anything to do with any of that. And every day I wonder what to do about any of that. I finally have to let it go and revel in who I am and how strong I am and how stunning and brilliant and creative and....It's just that I'm the only one who will ever know.

I am not wallowing in self-pity. On the contrary, I invite the adversity into my life as training for the even harder events that will ensue later. Every day is training for the next day, and I need all the training I can get. So I just have to write about all of it. Every day is an onslaught.

After the cancer forced me to come back to Michigan in 2013, it soon became apparent that I was going to be a parent. To my mother.

By 2015, at the age of 77, she had forgotten how to open the fridge (nor does she understand the word anymore) and put together a simple meal. Same for the oven, microwave, and coffeemaker. She was never any good at cooking anyway. She was always good at watching the news, though. She knew who the President was, when it was Obama, but not what year it was, or when her birthday is. She didn't brush her hair anymore. I took her to church and to choir and looked at her hair that she had not looked at. She had been sitting on the sofa all day, day after day, never looking in the mirror, and so the back of her head became a multi-directional mishmash. She didn't care. She didn't know. Part of me can't wait to not care too. But another part says, "Merry, you will be picking out your outfit and orchestrating your own memorial service when you are her age. And you will care how your hair looks. You will desperately care." I care now, why not then?

She is my only child. I am finally getting the experience of what it's like to have children. The truth is, I always knew I would be the one to care for my mother, as she was self-sacrificing to a fault, never looking out for her own interests or needs, and my father didn't look out for her much either. He didn't bother to pay into social security or Medicare. She taught English in 1959 and 1960. Years later, after following my father's career in science at MIT and as a professor at Notre Dame, she taught an environmental course for a few years at the local community college. This was the lifetime total of her paid work, not enough to qualify for Medicare. This woman held a Bachelor's degree in Communications from the University of Illinois, and single-handedly launched a marketing campaign for the fledgling organic beef farm my father started in 1980 in southwestern Michigan. Of all the things and of all the places! She spearheaded political activism with the League of Women Voters, started a "Citizens for Environmental Protection" group, and served on a panel in D.C. for the National Organic Standards Board. All that education, volunteer activity, unpaid research, and upstart bravado, but no Medicare. Luckily, the farm can still pay her bills, but only if she keeps the meager lifestyle to which she has become accustomed.

At 77, she spent her days floating between CNN, writing her "book," crosswords, Tetris, jigsaw puzzles, and pouring half a bag of cat chow on the front deck. She ingested nothing but raisin toast, orange juice, cheese, Barq's root beer, and chocolate, unless I forced her to eat something I cooked. She put on the same shirt every day. She asked me the same questions every day. "Do you come back over here after I go to bed?" *Yes, mother, I walk back and forth from the cabin all day and half the night.* Especially in the winter since I had to feed the fire in the basement. I walked from my cabin next door, the renovation project I was determined to take on after my divorce. I could not stand to allow it to fall to ruin. And there was the subliminal knowledge that she would need me there someday. Someday soon.

After living a full 10 years in California, the adjustment was tough. It still is. Ten years later, the place still needs work. And only a select few have ever been inside of it. Kind of like my vagina.

Since 2005, I have come and gone from the cabin for various far-flung endeavors, and each time I come back it is like a return to both a beginning and an end, a way of marking the chapters of my life. I step back in time and revisit my 16-year-old self as I dance on the exact same floor boards I did when *Flashdance* was all the rage. That teenager had wisdom beyond her years. Or else I am a thoroughly immature 50-something woman. I have talks with my 80-year-old self who has also been here all along, like the cobwebs. Each time I return, I unearth the baseboards of my identity, stripped down to the bare bones.

Am I just another crazy wannabe literary outcast in her far-flung cabin on an old organic farm?

Just like my mother?

Yes and no, I tell myself.

I was able to follow my zigzagging passions somehow wherever they led for pretty much my whole life. Some might envy me; others might pity me. I was shooting for the stars, but now even seemingly simple outcomes seem like impossible dreams. Am I really supposed to still be looking for Mr. Right? An adopted kid? A $60,000 income, a two-car garage, and a 55-inch TV? *I never knew I was supposed to want these things.* I already had most of those things with my first husband, but the price I paid was much higher than the value of the items themselves.

Driving around the small towns where I grew up, I gaze at the unchanged pockets of poverty. People are sitting on their sagging front porches. Some are making futile attempts to fix the siding, and the front yards are strewn with rusty bikes, cars, tires, wind catchers, and all manner of recyclables. And I think again about how you can't fix stupid. Am I a Republican now? We could throw money at some people all day and they would keep spending it on drugs and cars. But it's not just that—it's the reminder of the limits of money. That money itself will not solve problems, relieve loneliness, prevent child abuse or suicide, stop wars, or fix climate change. It is collective human will alone that may be able to do these things. How do we harness that?

Back to mom. I don't even know where all that other stuff came from. There were times in my life when I was catapulting from one bad decision to another potentially worse decision while she was the voice of reason that I tried to shut out. *What does this old lady know about my world?* Is that what my niece thinks about her mom and me? Is the world that different now than in the past? A kiss is still a kiss, isn't it?

And from this kiss, a life spills forth in all its glory, chaos, and exquisite potential. So much potential. So much scattering.

She ventures outside intermittently, wandering to the pond where her husband's ashes were scattered, or picking up pinecones for no apparent reason. She imagines that she is gardening, but she is just looking at what she planted years ago. Looking at me, what does she see? What kind of plant am I? Knowing that her memory of me is fading, I have to realize that she is the one person on this planet who has watched me grow from my beginning. Who will know me now? Who? Who? Who? Like the owls in my woods. Then I remind myself to strive not so much to be understood, but to understand.

What is it about the decline or death of a parent that makes the child feel they must do penance? The suffering of the parent means the child must follow suit? It's like paying back the parent for the suffering you caused them as a child. We will follow suit soon enough. We don't have to go looking for suffering. Maybe Alzheimer's is a blessing. It exists so you don't have to go around being haunted by your past for the rest of your fucking life.

When I went through cancer (again), I was terrified to think that I might die before her. Who would take care of her? My brothers? They lived nearby but rarely came to see her. It was partly my love for her that gave me a sense of purpose and a drive to stay alive. It was also all that unfinished business…all the projects that I had put off for so long because I was still too busy competing with 26-year-olds. In a strip club, no less. Yes, a post-menopausal, three-time-cancer-surviving stripper. Holy cow. That's either super tragic or devoutly to be wished for, depending on your point of view. Maybe that is the ultimate success for a woman: to look 30 at the age of 50! Well, I don't look 30, exactly… depends on the lighting.

After 5 years of taking care of her, I have decided maybe it's time to stop all the kvetching about how I am supposed to be someplace else, doing something else, and coming up with enough money to pay someone else to take care of her. I am doing what I am supposed to be doing when I am supposed to be doing it. At least for now. Acceptance of my true present place and moment is difficult. In America we only move forward. Looking back or being with the present is not allowed.

Listening to the spring peepers in the wetlands behind my cabin, I just hope that by striving to be myself in a world that does not favor that, I kind of did justice to what my parents tried to create: a business ahead of its time, and kids who swim upstream against all odds. Some have called me "Hurricane Merry." The only safe place is in the eye of the storm.

Time to go brush hair again…and deal with the starlings living above my back door. I will just bang on the wall to scare them off.

Credit cards. I love shuffling them around, running them up about halfway, paying them off right before the interest rate kicks in, gathering points. They think they will corner me one day, but I'm way ahead of them. I have no problem paying the transfer fees, but won't get caught dead paying any of that god damn interest. Why pay for stuff until you have to? So I screw around on Amazon looking for just the right protein powder, or researching the latest amazing skin care product.

Money is a loaded issue, though. That's why people who are loaded have so many issues. I usually call Citibank customer service to discuss ALL of my issues. It's cheap therapy...and you get what you pay for.

Speaking of therapy—

I just love the set of questions you get while going through security at Heathrow:

What did you do on your trip?

Who were you with?

Where did you stay?

What restaurants did you go to?

What do you do for a living?

What does your friend do for a living?

How long have you known him?

Where did you stay?

How long were you in...?

Do you have any hobbies?

Where do you live?

This guy was maybe Nigerian with a London accent. And I answered all his questions like I was being interviewed on Oprah. "Oh, I was with my old flame from junior high and we had *sex*! OMG that was the first time I had sex in 2 years! Because, see, I had cancer in 2013 and I went through some major depression and menopause, of course. But I got my book finished anyway and oh, do you want my card?"

No one had shown so much interest in me in a long time.

Lying. Let's talk about it. Or better yet, let's lie about it. We all do it. Not on purpose. We lie to others because we are lying to ourselves and we just don't realize it. We should all assume that at least half of what people tell us in person is false and that 80% of everything we read on the internet is also false. The stuff that is definitely true on the internet is...um, wait, there must be...I'm thinking...uh...oh, yes! The weather forecast is usually accurate. Sometimes.

We all think we are "good" people, not even knowing what that means. We think we are intelligent people, but that is also quite difficult to pin down with any certainty. I guess we could go off our SAT scores or remind ourselves that we graduated from a high-end university and so no matter what happened after that, we always assumed we were, in fact, intelligent, and furthermore, educated to a degree. Bachelor's, Master's, Ph.D— one of those degrees. We assume that most of the people with whom we interact daily are also "good" people and fairly intelligent as well. Except those other drivers on the road. They are all clownheads.

But some days, we all have this feeling that maybe...maybe we are not *that* good or maybe not *that* intelligent, after all. *Okay, maybe I am the only one who thinks this, because I like to try to be honest with myself, unlike some others who persist in lying to themselves.* Like I said, it's all relative. Our relatives are to blame for any of our own shortcomings. We did not choose them, but these people we lived with for the first 18 years of our lives had more influence on us than anyone else. I, for one, am still trying to understand this influence and what it means today, or what it should mean, if anything. But, anyway, my point is, the minute you assume that you are intelligent, you are probably missing something.

One night, I was falling asleep watching *Mrs. Doubtfire* on the sofa. At 12:30 a.m. I was thinking I needed chocolate, but also Imodium, because things just hadn't been the same since the damn colonoscopy. Then I had to write down my calorie count for the day, which I am sure I underestimated again. By 2 a.m., I was logging on to my online class to see if it was gonna be worth it, while thinking of what time I needed to get up. My cat was distracting me, so I had to lock it in the basement. I don't hesitate to highlight any and all of my human foibles and the existential morass that we all somehow wade through every day.

I went so far as to take a class to improve my stand-up routine, and the guy teaching the class commented that he thought I was trying to be a caricature of myself. *No, this is the real me.* This is either just how far gone I am or just how good I am. I am quite naturally a cartoon of myself.

A friend who had already made a bunch of money in finance told me about the equity he had gained on his house—and I began kvetching to myself about how I would never catch up with this person financially. Maybe I could inch up with net worth, but income-wise, it was doubtful. My only hope is just betting on myself. Even though I am a gambling woman, sometimes the odds overwhelm the psyche.

Money seems to be my prime focus right now. There is still so much to do, I don't have a clue how much time I have, and I barely know how to allocate and prioritize my limited funds. I keep running numbers over and over and coming up with crazy business ideas. Yoga yurts on the Interstate! A wearable moral compass! I am sure someone is going to take these ideas and run with them.

My friend knew what he wanted long ago and had a plan, while I just improvised my way through. The entertainment industry is a fickle mistress. I knew that. But I had to live an adventure and write about it, so perhaps others could learn from my experiences and challenges, regardless of how it all turned out. I never even had much of a financial plan at all until about 37, after the second bout with cancer, and when I realized I had to fix up the cabin by myself.

I have to just do what we all do. Do what I can with what I still have to work with. I keep my college writing to remind myself that I did have a brain at one point, and maybe still do, if I just keep digging for it... it's still here somewhere.

If I am out in the world too long, I become a diaspora of myself. Must have a centered spot. Right here in the place where I danced at 16.

I would rather have beautiful painful utter chaos than comfort and predictability.
I would rather struggle against all odds than have everything laid out for me.
I would rather have
Me.

Sometimes it just seems like if you look at someone's face long enough and hard enough, they can never die.

After opening up my own normally closed, catty, and chatty mind to other genuine voices, I regain respect for the superhuman act of a person attempting to capture their naked psyche on a page with something so confining as the English language. And by extension,

I regain my self-respect as I struggle in vain to not just connect with, not just "resonate with," but to literally merge my very essence with another psyche to the point of actually becoming part of another mind. Well, that sounds like I am making love to them. I am. I want my voice in this other person's head, in my friend's head as well as my enemy's head. Forever. Is this something good to want for others, or is it just evil? I'm worth it! Certainly, there are other voices that have merged with *my* head. Lots of voices. They are all yelling at me most of time.

It just seems so wrong. That all the striving and sweating and feeling and crying and dancing and thinking and working all leads to...death! What is that? Going to sleep and never waking up? Nothing. Darkness. No memory. No feeling. No sensation. No thought. The cessation of all that ever mattered to us. The cessation of us.

There must be a way around it, we tell ourselves. Some circumvention, some sidestepping, some dodging or ducking, fancy footwork, dancing...

No. The deadline approaches. Regardless.

"It's just like I remember it."

Is it really?

Does memory lie to us?

Does it make us feel like the past was this unbelievable flight of fantasy and today is just a weak reverberation of that? Is the present just an echo chamber of the past?

Probably.

Can we ever see things clearly?

Do we ever know who we are or who anyone else is?

In a word: No.

If it's all perception, then it all evaporates when we stop perceiving; when we shut down. We yearn for a sign that somehow we *matter,* in all contexts. We doubt that the people in our lives really know us at all.

I envy those who are not bothered by these thoughts.

People tell me I worry too much.

People tell me I am too hard on myself.

People tell me I obsess over my looks.

Or over money.

I am a woman.

I live in America.

This is what happens.

Write-ins 2016:

What the Fuck.

America is doomed.

You have got to be kidding me.

Nuke it.

Bite me.

Fuck off.

My dog Coco.

Oprah.

JFK: Why be biased against dead Presidents?

Me me me!!

CNN

Fox News

NPR

The 99%

Fidel Castro

My cat, Fozzy Bear

Power to the People

So I stood there in the terminal at O'Hare with some millennials around me who tried to be reassuring both to me and to some of the young women standing there. We were watching the most catastrophic thing imaginable as the election results dripped in like Chinese water torture from the Rust Belt states. Why wasn't my reliably Blue Michigan turning blue? Because I was. I was holding my breath. A racist sexist xenophobic classist revolting monstrous mouth breather who oozes the most grandiose attitude about him him him was winning an election for the President of what used to be the United States of America. Does he genuflect to his self-portrait every night? I could take an amalgamation of Reagan, Bush, and Romney altogether over this horror show.

And I guess that's how a lot of people were programmed to think about Hillary.

When the plane finally lifted off after a 3-hour delay from O'Hare for San Francisco, I looked out the window as my eyes welled up with tears. I thought I was going to be toasting champagne at the Napa Valley Film Festival after we had elected the first female President of the US. What happened? How could this be? How could I continue to live in a country with people who voted for that man?? It was as though 62 million people had just punched me in the gut. What kind of a person would vote for that? It's quite devastating to survive cancer and then look around and realize the cancer was the least of your problems.

After I woke up in California on November 9th, I texted and called every person I could think of to cry over the phone with them. I could not get out of bed. I finally got out of bed and made the first few steps towards facing the world, and then I would just break down again.

I cried for two hours in the hotel bathtub. It was like PTSD. I could not understand how even *one* person could hate Hillary *so much* that they would actually vote for *that man*. I never will. But I guess I was not exposed to the extreme vilifying process that the conservative media executed against her with great force and discipline. I did not even know of the existence of Breitbart until late in the campaign. I knew that watching Bill O'Reilly would just make me seethe, so when I heard about Breitbart, I knew it would make me hyperventilate. I never listened to Rush Limbaugh, either. It isn't so much what these people say. It's how. Well, it's both.

So after the election, I needed an antidote. I began reading *White Trash, Dark Money, Our Revolution*, and Gloria Steinem's memoir all at once, dipping in and out of the *New York Times*, *The Guardian*, and the *Washington Post*, plus intermittent bits of CNN…and finally laughing with Bill Maher and *SNL* every week. Of course, there is always NPR in the car. This media mix seemed at once thorough, but maybe a bit of an echo chamber. I tried looking at Breitbart and Fox News once in a while, to do my best to avoid the echo chamber, but found that I just could not stomach it. There is only so much exposure to a stomach-churning perspective that a person can tolerate. I have decided that if I simply keep up with headlines and listen to what people say and watch what they do, I do not need to listen to sixteen analysts droning on about the same events every night. I can listen to the analysis in my own head. Along with all the other voices.

I was concerned about this country before November 8th, 2016. Now I feel like everything that was still quite good about this country is in serious jeopardy. We had freedom of speech and a free press. We had at least the illusion of transparency. No accountability, but at least we knew about the shit people were pulling even though they were thumbing their noses at the rest of us. *Yeah, what are you gonna do about it? We got Citizens United, nyah nyah nyah.* The internet was there for all of us to do our supposedly independent homework and thought process. But now the media is owned by six corporations. Might be five at this point. And these conglomerates infiltrate all the main sources of news.

This is a war between good and evil, and evil does not care about facts. It laughs at them and throws money at them to make them go away. Then it replaces them with lies. Money talks. It screams. It whispers. It seduces. And people, votes, power, corporations, and whole institutions can be bought and sold. America has in fact been bought and sold many times over. Well, the first "purchase" was actually theft. Let's face it. Theft and genocide are the twin towers of colonialism. We are not safe. The planet is not safe. We know why JFK was assassinated. And why Trump won.

You talkin' to me? Every word Trump has ever said is a fighting word. I take it personally on so many levels, as an American, as a human being, and as a woman. It's not just about him being racist or sexist or anti-Semitic or xenophobic. It's about the fact that he looks down his nose at *everyone* who is not a white male conservative billionaire. He only cares about you if you are his gender, in his economic class, and in his political camp. Every speech I ever heard from him was pure self-idolatry and pissing on everyone and everything else that is not *him* or *about him.* Even in the debates, he rarely made eye contact with his opponents, just giving sidelong glances out the corner of his beady little lizard eyes.

Everything that happens to an individual American happens to America. We are supposed to be a beacon of hope. A light in the dark tunnel. The Statue of Liberty is our welcome sign. *She* is raising light and carrying a book. *She.* The hope of generations and the wisdom of the ages.

I have always believed that there are others out there like me: concerned with the broader society and the world as a whole, but lacking resources and a support system. If we could all just join together somehow. Who is really motivated to level the playing field except those on the low end of it? Why would those on the high end want to be on the same level as everyone else? They don't. That's why they fly business class.

People tell you that you can only get rich by doing what you love. *This makes no sense.* You might love yo-yoing and spirographs. No one is going to pay you to do these things unless you are SOOOOOO amazing at doing them *and* you figure out how to package and market these talents and go viral on YouTube. So maybe it is true. You have to LOVE something SO MUCH that you will do *whatever it takes* to make money doing it. This is how good parents feel about their kids. They will do *whatever it takes* to provide the best life they can for their kids.

Actually, American media did impress on my young brain that there are other routes to social influence besides accumulating great wealth: become a celebrity or a political figure. Make history or become a "star." Preferably both. Either of these is a great position from which to push for positive social change. Not fame for its own sake or my own sake, but for the sake of a microphone to speak to millions about the causes that I cared about. But what's this? *Everyone* has a microphone now. There's a big one sitting on my desk right now and I don't even know what to do with it. Everyone is clamoring to be heard.

At times, I thought Trump was just a front man for the media, a lightning rod to attract viewers who wanted to hear and see what bullshit and vitriol he would spew next. I had to think that there was some quid pro quo going on. What would motivate a man who is only about himself to keep coming up with such outlandish hateful rhetoric and going in front of actual TV cameras and unleashing all of it? I guess a man like that could be motivated just by getting attention. He could go home every night and watch himself and drown in the sound of his own ugly grating voice.

I wonder what it must be like to be a man. To walk into a room and just get respect automatically. To not have to prove myself. Again. And again. And again. And again. And again. To not be judged by my hair or shoes or dress size or Botox or lack thereof. No, it's not penis envy. It's *person* envy. I am a *person* trapped in a woman's body. To be a person first instead of a *woman* first. To not have this question about what it's like to be a *female* _____. Perhaps people are starting to ask what's it like to be a male flight attendant, but I have never heard this question myself.

I should never look at stats on wealth and income in America. It just drives me to eat gummy bears. There are people out there making *how much money??* It's just beyond my comprehension. How? How does anyone make over a million a year? Or $40 million? (I think that is a one-time thing. Some buy-out, golden parachute, or hedge fund deal, right?) But why should I care? I am not that money motivated. I mean, if it takes millions to get my books in front of millions of eyeballs, then maybe.

I guess the only consolation is knowing that the group churns over. There's a revolving door at the millionaire club. Right? It's a different group of people each year. Right? Billionaires, on the other hand, tend to stay billionaires. But not Trump. I don't think he actually is, he's just a wannabe. Anyway, just makes the rest of us seem like chumps.

Depression increases in proportion to the amount of exposure to the media and the bombardment of how we should all strive endlessly to be part of the upper crust. But the pieces of the upper crust whom I have come across did not impress me. They made me want to run screaming from the building or house or plane. *An asshole is an asshole regardless of his money.* Trump proves this beyond any shadow of a doubt and maybe America will somehow learn a lesson through all of this. Money never has, does not, and never will, make someone *right*.

"Just marry a rich man" was the mantra I was repeatedly told in younger years. Why? If he holds the purse strings and I don't make even 20% of what he does, what's to keep him from making my life a living hell? Power imbalances in relationships are the primary cause of divorce. It's not "irreconcilable differences." It's the fact that one party feels *they are entitled to look down on the other*. It's the fact that one party feels like a prisoner or a slave, even. It's the fact that one party feels that the other is not pulling their weight. Resentment. Blame. Lack of communication. *Not accepting and respecting the humanity of the other.* And that is how everything is politics. The quest for power is in every human relationship. Who is the Dominant? Who is the Submissive? Two people cannot lead at the exact same time.

This is America. I was told that I too could be a billionaire, *if I just work hard enough.* (Actually, no one ever told me that I could be a billionaire, just to marry one.) What *kind* of work? How hard is hard enough? The thing is, I could meritocracy my ass off and still never be a billionaire. Because my daddy was not rich enough, I did not marry rich, I did not go to business school (no one told me this was a prerequisite), and I am not connected to any of the "right" people. I will therefore never live on 5th Avenue or in Malibu. (Okay, maybe if I don't die before 70, I might still have some sort of chance, so I will keep dreaming.)

And then there was this altruistic streak in me that made me not exactly *laser focused* on becoming rich, but rather helping others through education and preserving my own freedom of expression and mobility. I figured that a full-time job would tie me down and make me shut up. Yes. It would. But it might get me more money. How much? Not *power* money. Power to sway elections and legislation. That's the power that *matters.*

Yet freedom of expression can be a powerful thing. I never would have had a chance at Harvard. With my mouth and the ADHD...I would have been their worst nightmare of a student.

I read the book *White Trash,* and it only underscored what most of us don't want to acknowledge: There is not and never was a classless society in America. Britain dumped their criminals and homeless here, in the swamp, and then sent over a few upper-class people to manage them and get rid of the natives (drain the swamp)—the usual twin goals of colonization and gentrification. Yes, I said that again. Most things are still determined at birth. The myth of upward mobility just keeps people struggling and feeling bad about themselves.

I hope my richest friend gets to be a billionaire one day. Then I can at least say I know one. Then maybe I would not be white trash. No, no, I am not white trash because I read books like *White Trash*. And I went to college, dammit. But I don't know, look at my slippers. You can tell a lot about a person from their slippers.

The free market has no conscience. Great freedom requires even greater responsibility. Capitalists are not responsible to anyone except shareholders. Giving free rein to the powerful means the powerless will die. *Self-regulation??* You're kidding me. *Yeah, yeah, we are going to make up our own rules and then decide if we are following them.* What if a football game had only the players themselves as referees?

"Liberty for wolves is death for lambs." Isaiah Berlin.

Trump is only renting the White House, but he thinks he can buy it, and acts like he owns it already. Hillary was right when she talked about the vast right-wing conspiracy a few years back. It had nothing to do with Bill's indiscretions. It had to do with what we are seeing now: the dark money has been fueling this movement for decades. It is now up to the American people to fully understand what is at stake. There is no "justice for all" in a system taken over by market forces that have no justice embedded in them. Some will say: "It can't happen here." It can. And it has, to a large extent.

Remember the boiling frogs? The only way fascism will not take over America is because we, the segment of the American people who know fascism when they see it, will stand in front of the steamrollers.

It has always been this way. The oligarchy has always been with us, attempting to bulldoze everything the little people have left. What can we do for our country? We can stand up and speak for what we still value: protecting the planet and the people who live on it, even if some of those people are oblivious to the forces that are aligned to destroy all that they may have.

The elite are only elite if they realize they are fallible. Believing oneself to be beyond reproach is known as a fatal flaw. We each have a fatal flaw. If someone who has made a lot of money thinks he or she is an expert in everything, that is ego talking, not wisdom. Because what does it mean to be "elite"? Is it enough to simply be born into the upper class? Is it enough to have the best education? I have known people who were highly educated and shrewd but looked down their nose at almost everyone else. This is the fascist attitude. Or maybe it's the rest of us letting ourselves believe the hype. Those who think they know everything are the most sadly mistaken. Those of us who admit our weaknesses are actually the strongest. Honesty takes bravery. To admit insecurity instead of acting as if one has all the answers is one true sign of basic humanity, the foundation of strength and of character. And of course, that's *me*. Yes, I am better than everyone else.

Oh shit, am I lapsing into didactic territory? Oh well.

The struggle between two opposing sets of facts is real. Each side has its own think tanks and stats paid for by each political camp. This is death to a healthy democracy, and I can only hope that the next generations will make it their business to reveal the truth with no agenda. Humans With Internet is a new-fangled amalgamation. Technology is a *tool* for humans, not a *replacement* for humans. Ultimately, however, all intelligence is artificial. Doubt is still salvation.

Jesus was

a bastard

a vagabond

born into poverty

born in a barn

a gangster

a kick ass fisherman

a long-haired radical

friends with criminals

convicted for speaking his mind

punished for criticizing the powers that be

a change agent

damn brave

in love with everyone

a community organizer.

I do not think anyone should even be able to enter into public service unless they have experienced suffering and adversity. A person can hardly understand something that they haven't experienced, and if they don't understand it, how can they do anything about it?

Cases in point:

- If you have never been discriminated against, how can you fully understand what discrimination means?

- If you have never been in poverty, how can you fully understand what poverty means?

- If you have never been bullied, how would you know how that can affect a person for life?

- If you have never been through a life-threatening experience, how would you ever understand what that feels like?

- If you have never been abused or abandoned, you would have no sense of how that feels.

The experience of adversity creates empathy.

Climate March, 2017 Washington, DC

I found out about this march from a certain talk show on HBO. And I knew I had to go.

I was trying to find the Michigan Climate Action Network but gave up and just meandered around Capitol Hill and made my way through the park over to Third and Jefferson where the march was supposed to start. A climate change march with temps reaching up into the 90s at the end of April seemed all too ironic. Sweat started dripping as I watched more and more people gather. About one-third were older and two-thirds were younger than I. There was a pre-parade vibe as I sought out shade. With the drum beats and marching band instruments, it also felt a bit like a high school football game. This was organized. Everyone was a team.

The signs were so creative and most of them were hilarious, referring to Trump's tiny hands, Trump's love for Putin, the hatred of fascism, the love for the planet, and distrust of this tyrant.

Freedom to fuck over the populace — aka the subjects.

I will never understand why Republicans expect Americans to trust corporate America rather than their own government. If you advocate for the "free market" over everything else, that is what you are advocating. Just trust AT&T. I mean, what's not to trust? The government is supposed to protect the American people not just from foreign enemies, but from domestic predators who take advantage of those less advantaged.

We have met the enemy and he is us.

Holy shit. I'm in my 50s and I'm not a billionaire yet and I'll be honest, I am a little worried because…it is possible that I might NOT become a billionaire. (gasp)

No no no, we're not gonna go there.

And then I think about the fact that so many people, no matter how much money they have, are always going to be insecure, like you know who. He's not a Koch brother, he's just Fred Trump's son.

PART V
Bouncing Back Again

In 2013, I honestly thought I was going to die within a couple of years, so I did spend a good sum of money on the bucket list. Five years later, I'm still here. Well, at least I worked ahead. Miracles never cease. But this is rather awkward. It's like dealing with the world from a reincarnated state, and you don't really know what state it is or what state you're in.

How to jump-start this woman's life after so many near deaths? If you're like me, a neurotic, narcissistic, insecure older woman, you pick up where you left off by:

- Spending inordinate amounts of time on Realself.com

- Having neurotic consults with cosmetic doctors in four states

- Estimating how long recovery times will be

- Blindly applying for Master's programs with no recent accomplishments on the naked resume

- Pouring over job postings trying to decipher the language in the job descriptions

- Showing up at networking sessions with recent marketing grads I can barely follow

- Going to the gym with no particular plan of action

- Mulling over and over whether to start dating online

- Attempting an online class only to withdraw in frustration at the lack of support

- Taking crazy road trips, thinking each time will be the last

- Comparing myself to everybody everywhere

Girls, remember when you used to book a flight for yourself and have this fleeting romantic anticipation that you might meet someone special at some point on the trip? That you would get seat 23B and Mr. Right would be in 23A-mazing, and then your "real life" would finally begin? Or that maybe you would go out for a drink and meet this wonderful guy at the bar and find out that all your hobbies and political beliefs were perfectly aligned AND he made you laugh? Yeah.

No, I can't remember either. YOU can't even remember and you're probably a 28-year-old hottie. At least I hope I am reaching some 20-somethings with this opus.

A-part-ment: a part of the cement

Being an older version of yourself and returning to places that you lived when you were a younger version is like being a stranger in an even stranger land. It's not the way you remember it, and even if it is, you're not the same person remembering it anymore. Newsflash: I am not the person I was when I was 28. But that 28-year-old keeps harassing me and cajoling me and whining about the fact that she never got what she wanted when she wanted it. Am I supposed to feel sorry for her? Or am I supposed to just try to keep setting her straight as to why things are the way they are now? And it may be that what she wanted when she was 28 wasn't even what she *really* wanted, period. Maybe it takes a lifetime to know what you really want. Are women more guilty of not knowing what they want than men? Maybe it's because women are sent more conflicting and varied messages about what they are supposed to want and be. Do I want to be someone's hero or do I just want to be the prettiest girl in the airport terminal? How about both? Once a girl retires from making a living off relative youth and relative good looks, what does she...do?

I keep going back to this ridiculous line of thought that tells me if I get a full-time job I will therefore have given up on all of my dreams and I will never be able to accomplish any of the things that I really care about and I'll just be stuck in a really crappy job for the rest of my life. I assume all jobs are crappy because all the jobs I have ever had have been crappy. I don't see a job as a financial stepping stone. I see it as the fast track towards getting fired. Kind of like relationships are a stepping stone to break-ups. And marriage is a direct route to divorce.

Do I really want to go through all that—*again*? Does anyone? Why do people remarry? Is the fear of growing old alone that strong? Would you like to age peacefully, or with someone squawking in your ear?

I choose not to go to weddings because I don't believe in divorce. OMG, am I being too cynical?

I really am trying to let go

- of the need to feel like I am or have to be attractive to men

- of being a people pleaser

- of seeing both my age and my gender as impediments in every aspect of my life (even though they are)

- of my parents

- of my habit of never making real plans, but just "enacting experiments"

- of seeing everything as "material" instead of *my actual life*

Unfortunately, it seems like all of this is baked into my psyche, and if you stick a fork in that, you'll hit a wall of denial almost immediately. It's just thick enough to hold back the river of dread.

Do I need Adderall?

How do I know if I am overestimating or underestimating myself?

I don't know.

So I will just

take another road trip.

ROAD TRIP Jan 2017

After a rainy drive, arrived in beautiful Airbnb house 100 years old in San Luis Obispo.

SLO rocks: all the houses are small and old. Like me.

Two massages in Santa Barbara

Yoga class in Santa Barbara

Went to show benefiting the ACLU in Los Angeles and got my book into the hands of a certain high-level producer. I am so sure he appreciated my ambushing him behind the theater wearing bear paw boots and calling him by his first name like we were old pals.

Yoga class in San Luis Obispo

Hot Springs mineral bath at Avila Beach

Avila Beach sea caves

Winetasting at Cambria

Blue Dolphin Inn where I spent two nights.

Walked up the road at Ragged Point. Could not drive all the way to Big Sur because of all the rain and mud slides.

Saw sea elephants while running near San Simeon.

Drove PCH from Cambria to Manhattan Beach in cloudy rainy weather. But I could still see the ocean.

Checked into hotel and danced in the empty gym.

Consult with cosmetic surgeon (hey, I'm in California, after all).

Got a "little" Botox (hey, I'm in California after all).

Drove to another Airbnb house (more like a mansion) in Koreatown, used as a movie set periodically.

Did yoga (mostly corpse pose) in her in-home yoga studio and enjoyed the airy upstairs apartment.

Next day, drove across town to the Doubletree, dumped my stuff, and joined the Women's March at Pershing Square.

Headed to Las Vegas the next day to see friends and return to Red Rocks conservation area.

Then took a "slight" detour down to Tucson to check out the Miraval resort.

Took one day to explore the Sonoran Desert.

After stopping in Boulder a few days, I began the long boring trek back to Michigan.

Had a discussion of politics with the front desk manager at a Hampton Inn in Iowa.

It was good to be back in an actual house that is exactly the way I like it.

And good to see mom again, no matter how confused she is.

How many people manage to hang onto their childhood home? It just seems like I should hang onto it if at all possible. I mean, come on, the place is immortalized in my first book. Once you sell any *particular* thing, you will never get that exact thing back. Is it wrong to become attached to any material thing? It is impossible not to, if one has lived a number of years and has any sentiment at all. I still have my Raggedy Ann doll. I still have my iMac circa 2002 with the round base and chrome arm. That is still the best computer design ever. Too bad I can't unlock the File Vault on it. Have to work on that.

2032. If I am alive then, I will be 67 years old. 2032. I just sit here and look at that year and cannot believe I will actually live to see it. When I was 30, I thought 60 was unlikely. Now it's only eight years from now. *Eight!!* All because of medical technology and the will to live.

Perhaps maturity finally takes hold when one realizes that they too will get old and will, one day—die. Yes, the choices are either maturity or sheer panic at the fact that there is no way to recover all those lost years. I'm sure I can do both. I'm good at multitasking.

The victim mentality: who is not a victim of something? I think I have been exploited by insincere men my whole life (or maybe I'm the insincere one). I think sexism has affected every aspect of my life. Most men are sexist and think they aren't. I am probably racist and I think I'm not so.... Shit, could I be sexist too? Oh, no. Sexism is only possible in men.

VICTIMHOOD

- Victim of sibling rivalry. Possibly partly my own fault.

- Victim of misleading advertising. I was led to believe that America is the greatest country in the world and that anyone can accomplish anything here. Even a girl.

- Victim of my own neuroses.

- Victim of guilt.

- Victim of cancer.

- Victim of a society that only cares how much money you have, who your parents are, and where you live.

- Victim of being short.

- Victim of not being thin (enough).

- Victim of high prices.

- Victim of peer pressure.

- Victim of hormones.

- Victim of Subway sandwiches.

- Victim of car payments. (Oh, I bought the car. My fault.)

- Victim of student loans. (Oops, my fault too, for getting an education.)

- Victim of procrastination.
- Victim of credit cards. (I only got one so I could buy groceries.)
- Victim of interest rates.

"I know just how you feel."

No, you don't. No human being can possibly fully understand how another human being feels, unless you can shrink yourself down into a nanobot and implant yourself into another human's brain. We are alone in our feelings. Just like we are alone in death. And birth. Well, we aren't alone, we just don't recognize anybody, at both of those points.

Yoga is basically nap time for adults. You remember in kindergarten we used to all go get our mats or our blankies and have a nap at like 2 o'clock? That's because the teachers were exhausted, not us. We were just lying there looking at each other and giggling. I remember spreading out the blanket on a cold concrete floor. This was preparation for a hard life. But these days in yoga class, when we are in corpse pose, that's it, lights out, I'm going to sleep. And at my age, it really is hard to listen to some 20-year-old giving exercise instructions—to me, someone who used to teach AEROBICS. Makes me want to bitch slap the yoga girl.

You get to middle-age and you realize that you have this entire empty continent in your head. All that empty space used to be filled with thoughts about sex or, in the woman's case, *relationships*. I mean, any and all available space was jam-packed with sex when you were younger. Now there's a huge barren attic in your head and you think *wow I should put something here*. I should get some furniture up in this Vacant Real Estate in my head. And that is the order of life: Sex. Then furniture.

Another thing I'm really tired of are those people who tell me that such and such a class or procedure or speaker or book or podcast or *experience* will "change my life." A fucking heart attack will change my life. I don't need to go looking for somebody or something else to change my life. It's an insult to even be saying this to anyone because you're insinuating that there is something *wrong* with their life. Fuck you. Nothing wrong here. Depression is my default state of being as it probably is for most people.

And that is a major problem in America: We cannot leave anything well enough alone. Everything has to be changed or rearranged or improved or made over or upgraded or renovated or otherwise fucked with. Let's try a novel approach and just leave things alone. Let the untamed remain untamed. Except for the airports: they do need some upgrades.

So anyway, I went to a shrink. Yeah, we did a whole bunch of tests so I can find out what I was supposed to be in life, what my true calling actually was. And maybe I have some disabilities!! Then I can get a job based on my disability.

There are two problems I have with standardized tests:

1. the standards

2. the tests

Ho Hos, Dingdongs, Susie Qs, and who is this *Little Debbie? Tootsie roll*?? These all sound like porn titles. How old is this little Debbie? And where is Little Johnnie? And what is up with the *Three Musketeers,* may I ask?

I asked the cashier at the convenience store in Nebraska if she thought "ho hos" was a rather misogynistic term for junk food. She just looked at me with a blank stare. Then she started giggling at my quizzical look. She honestly did not know what misogynistic meant. She was straight off the reservation. Right then and there I decided I needed to move to Nebraska and teach English and absolutely include that word in all the vocabulary lists.

Women literally walk through the world sizing up other women:

Well, she might be prettier than me, but oh how shallow she is.

Well, she might be more educated than me, but she's fat.

Well, she might make more money than I do, but she's not funny.

She's thinner than me, but she has no boobs.

She's got longer hair, but I have a prettier face.

Not one is as funny or as deep as I am!!!

(Well, maybe a couple…but my boobs are bigger.)

Etc.

Sad. And maybe this is only me doing this, which is tragic.

I have detected a disturbing phenomenon in so-called creative people: Every creative person views their life as "material". Like it's not really happening. Rather, it's just going to be something amazing to write about or it's just going to give you so much more empathy for the human condition and your writing is just going to be all that much better because of it, when in reality, your life is a fucking train wreck and you're just jumping out of the train to watch the crash, to watch the flames rise higher and higher into the sky.

It's called dissociation.

Speaking of wrecks:

It jumped. It just committed suicide right there on Decatur Road. *Or did I commit murder? No, it was my car, not me.* Bam! "Oh, shit! I am hitting a...Jesus, I just hit a deer!" Bam. There was no time to brake or swerve. She leaped directly in front of the right headlamp. It was stunning. She flew through the air, and my car kept going. Why did she kill herself? *Why did I kill her?* Why at that very second on that exact road at that exact location did she decide to leap in front of my Prius? What was so important on the other side of that road? *What was so important that I had to intrude on her territory?* What were the odds that I was going to work on that route at that instant? I only took the backroads route to Kalamazoo to save myself five minutes in getting to l-94. *Am I not going to make it to work? No No No!* And what was her last thought?

It was a frigid December night on a pitch black country road, and as I pulled off, I could not see the damage initially. Then I lowered my eyes to just above the dashboard and saw the jagged edge of the crumpled hood. It never even crossed my mind that I might be hurt or might have been hurt. Nope. I just wanted to get to that damn strip club. After all, I had put in the hair and makeup time. I was not worried about the deer either. The carcass had landed down the road and was dimly visible in the light from one headlamp.

After shutting off the engine, I exhaled and stared at the hood again. I opened the door and my bearpaw bootie met the cold Michigan pavement. An image of Huntington Beach, California, flashed through my head. I walked around the front of the car and...*holy*...My beautiful green otherwise perfect condition but high mileage 2007 Toyota Prius, which I had bought new right after my dad passed, was demolished on the right corner and missing that headlight, like somebody had given it a black eye in a boxing ring. The radiator was concave and oozing, and the hood and bumper looked as if Goliath had intercepted my car from a slingshot. *This would not have happened if I still lived in Orange County, California.* Lots of things would not have happened if I still lived in Orange County, California.

Well, there goes my financial plan. Wait. Wait. I have insurance! I raised my arms towards the sky, like the scene in *Shawshank*. Yes! I knew I was covered for animals, because I kept hitting raccoons, and even they can destroy your bumper.

Okay, think. Put on your Big Girl Pants. This is nothing compared to cancer. AAA...

It seemed drivable. I mean, for a while. But there was a burning odor. I was not going to make it to my destination. A stray SUV pulled over, and a lady asked if I was okay.

"Yes, thanks, but my car is not. And the deer is definitely not. But I have triple A so..."

She drove off, and I trudged back to my trashed Prius, inspected it with the flashlight from the iPhone, sighed, and got back in. I pushed the button, and it started. It sounded fine. I slowly turned around in the road and chugged back to where I'd come from, catching whiffs of burning radiator as I went. After about a mile, I knew I had to park it and flee the scene. But not on the side of the road, like some discarded

Coke bottle. The Center for Aging was the only place with a parking lot for miles around. I made it there in about a half mile.

I was still determined to get to work. There was no choice but to call... "the guy next door."

This former Marine lived in the old stone library house on Library Road a few minutes from my itty bitty green cabin in the woods. It was thusly known as "the library house," since it had actually been a library in the 1930s. It even had names of authors engraved on the stones. When I had met him ten years prior, that was the most impressive thing about him—the house. Certainly not the former Marine status, which he never let anyone forget. The only hoodie he ever wore had "Marines" emblazoned on it. He had helped me out with various emergencies and I did not want my family to find out.

I texted him.

I hit a deer.

I sent him a picture.

He called me.

"How is the deer?" he asked.

"Yeah, yeah, real funny. The thing just jumped out of nowhere, like it knew I was there and it wanted to kill itself. The thing is, I still want to get to work. I put make up on, damn it."

"Where are you?"

"I am at the Center for Aging, of all places. I am never going this way to work again. At least not in the dark."

He showed up about 15 minutes later. I was standing in front of the car, thinking he would get out and have a look. No. He stayed in his Explorer, and when I did not hop in immediately, he stuck his head out the window.

"C'mon, let's get out of here."

"Don't you want to see what happened?"

He scrambled out. He was wearing the Ranger hoodie as usual, jeans that were a bit too long but somehow did not drag, and black SAS shoes. His receding hairline made his forehead look bigger and bigger each time I saw him. Somehow this only increased his appearance of volatility, like he was always ready to erupt. His head tilted one way and then the other as if he were cocking his ear towards a sound coming from a particular direction. Each time I looked him in the eye, I always thought I saw a micro-lightning strike.

"Oh, yeah, you creamed it."

"Do you think they can fix it?"

"I don't know. You called AAA, right?"

"Yeah, but they told me they couldn't get here till tomorrow."

"Ok, well, let's go. Nothing else you can do now."

The hour drive to Kalamazoo was a melange of me freaking out about whether or not the car was totaled and him irking me with his Republican bias, which he always managed to fit in edgewise into any exchange.

There is something both decent and indecent about a guy who will drive his sometime-girlfriend to the strip club to work. I decided it was mostly decent. This time.

Typical text message volley when attempting to date at 50. The baggage keeps getting heavier.

Texting starts with TM (Typical Man).

TM: I AM IMPRESSED; YOU'RE DOING WHAT IS NECESSARY TO SUCCEED, SURVIVE, MOVE FORWARD, AND BE HAPPY. NOTHING WRONG WITH THAT. THERE ARE A LOT OF MEN ONLINE AND BASED ON THE AMOUNT OF EMAILS YOU'RE GETTING, I BET YOU COULD FIND ONE WHO IS YOUR TYPE AND MIGHT BE THE ONE YOU'RE LOOKING FOR.

MB: Yes, but I have to be ready for whatever is going to happen. You just never know. I worry about money constantly. I have lost a lot of earning time. I probably should not be looking for a man. I have just been alone for so long I just thought maybe I could simply find a friend. But like the movie says, "Men and women can never be friends." I will probably spend the rest of my life in this cabin trying to write something, just like my mom did in the farmhouse.

I don't know if I can handle everything I'm dealing with and still have to deal with.

TM: PUT YOURSELF DOWN LESS AND GO FIND YOUR PRINCE.

MB: There are no princes online, just this princess.

TM: SAD FOR YOU THEN.

MB: No, it's sad for them. I just gave myself a compliment. You know the writing was on the wall a long time ago, don't you? A low self-esteem but fairly pretty girl with no money and no connections thinks she can go out into the world by herself and she gets treated like shit everywhere she goes. She does crazy things for love and money because she's desperate and she doesn't want to go back home because her father is a jerk. She realizes that America is about class and money and she does not have enough of either one.

TM: YOU DO HAVE ISSUES DEAR. AT LEAST YOU KNOW WHAT THEY ARE. BUT SEX SEEMS UNIMPORTANT TO YOU.

MB: Sex is important to me, but I have to forget about it because I'm postmenopausal. To be honest, things don't work the way they used to. And besides, I would never have sex with anybody I've known for less than three months. Are you just looking for sex? Sex is always there, you don't have to talk about it.

TM: PASSION IS THE KEY TRAIT IN PEOPLE LIKE ME; WE DON'T DO ANYTHING WE DON'T HAVE A PASSION FOR. MONTHS BEFORE YOU HAVE SEX? WOW, IT SEEMS LIKE YOU ARE LIVING IN THE ANCIENT TIMES. NO, I AM NOT JUST LOOKING FOR SEX, MOST INTELLIGENT MEN DON'T DO THAT, BUT I AM NOT INTERESTED IN A NUN.

MB: I guess I should put a disclaimer on my profile: Note: this woman is not willing to have sex until she has known someone for at least three months. I have to be in love with someone and I do not fall in love at first sight, I have to get to know someone before I'm going to do anything intimate and if you expect more than that, you're only going to be having sex with easy women.

I'm interested in a relationship and that takes time. Sex has been the root cause of all the bad decisions I have made in life. Sex is nothing but trouble for a woman.

TM: THAT IS NOT THE ISSUE. TODAY IS THE FIRST DAY OF THE REST OF YOUR LIFE—ONLY THAT COUNTS. I CAN TELL I'M NOT YOUR TYPE FROM ALL THE REMARKS YOU HAVE MADE THE TWO TIMES WE HAVE BEEN TOGETHER IN PERSON, SO THAT'S WHY I SAID YOU SHOULD GO AND FIND YOUR PRINCE.

MB: What did I say that means you're not my type? Just because I may act like I can't stand to be upstaged by anybody? Why can't I have a huge ego? Most men do.

TM: IF MEN EVEN READ YOUR WHOLE PROFILE, THEY WILL TRY TO GO FOR THE TIMETABLE, BUT IF THEY HAVE PLENTY OF OTHER OPTIONS, THEY WILL LEAVE. GOOD LUCK WITH THAT. I'VE ALWAYS WANTED TO BE CRAZY ABOUT SOMEONE AND ADDICTED TO THEM. I HAVE NOT EVEN GOT CLOSE.

MB: I have not gotten close either. That only happens in the movies. Furthermore, I am not an "option." I am not an addiction. I am a human being.

TM: YOU'RE SPLITTING WORDS.

MB: No, I'm not. You said "option," like picking a cell phone plan or a flight. Option A, B, C, D. What kind of a way is that to think about humans? You're proving my point that all men are sexist, even if they think they're not. I am not a drug habit either. That's an addiction.

TM: BY "OPTIONS" I DID NOT MEAN THAT THEY ARE NOT HUMAN BEINGS, I JUST MEAN THERE ARE OTHER HUMAN BEINGS MORE IN LINE WITH WHAT THEY ARE LOOKING FOR. EVERYBODY IS CHASING SOMEONE BETTER.

MB: And by "better" you mean someone who will fuck more? Someone thinner, younger, sexier? It's not about the person then, it's only about how much sex, how much youth, and how skinny. Who cares? Almost any vagina will do. Sad.

TM: I'M NOT SURE WHAT BETTER MEANS; OBVIOUSLY IT'S SOMETHING DIFFERENT FOR EVERYBODY. A LOT OF PEOPLE USE THAT PHRASE "THE ONE".

MB: It's a bullshit phrase. How does anybody know when they have met "the one"? How does anybody know how to even search for "the one"? The "better" person is the one person who will simply stick with you no matter what. Look, I haven't had sex for a long time. Because I don't have a partner and I have been too busy to look for one. Do you think I'm just supposed to fuck anybody just for the sake of fucking? I am free from that. Unlike some people.

You know how after you haven't had sex for a really *really* long time (like over 2 years) and you somehow start thinking that nobody's having sex and you forget that the world actually does go on without you and people are still having sex. It's just that *you* aren't.

And then you finally get out there again and you actually somehow have sex again and it's just like this shock to the system to realize that people still do that stuff. And that they have been doing it the *whole entire time* that you have not been doing it.

And you thought it was antiquated kind of outmoded, replaced by Google and porn somehow. Nope.

You are the one who is antiquated.

You are the one who is outmoded.

You are the one who has replaced sex with Google.

You are the one who has been replaced.

Random thoughts when starting to date at 52, after being alone for 10 years:

It's OK.

He hasn't run away yet.

Communication level is at about a B+.

He's just not ready for all my drama and complexity.

Like who is?

I do need to get a handle on my insecurities and neuroses.

That's the problem with letting somebody into your life.

They're going to tell you stuff that they see, and it goes both ways.

You have to look both ways.

It's not just a two-way street, it's a two-way mirror.

Yet all mirrors are seen through a haze of media-induced distortion.

We see people the way we have been molded to see them.

Nobody's perfect, and I've never been able to accept my own imperfections, let alone somebody else's.

My god, are you kidding??

But that's what I'm realizing: when I date somebody, I am taking somebody else along with me on a trip through my brain, like they're a pinball too. And now this other unfortunate person is going to know how it feels to be that pinball, but I think that he'll get into it and it will become a fun game…

In conversation, he will realize that I'm going to branch out from a subject and go out on a limb, but I'm always going to come back, and the tree is going to keep growing up, and he'll be cool with it. Sure.

SIGH.

I should just stay in my cabin and wait for problems to come to me instead of going out into the world looking for them. Just doing things because what the fuck, I'm bored?? Going out and trying to *date* again? Are you fucking kidding me?

Trouble will find you soon enough. You don't have to go looking for it. Dating at this age, or any age, is just inviting trouble into your life.

Laying out the red carpet. *Come on in. Cause some trouble.* I just don't know if I have it in me to go through all this, and if I really think I'm going to find some guy who's actually going to treat me like a queen for the rest of my life and maybe even *marry* me, what kind of fantasy world am I living in?

What shitty chick flick do I think I'm in? Um…*Pretty Woman* was about a YOUNG woman.

And she was tall and had long hair and she was gorgeous. You think this is worth it? To find "the one" at THIS POINT IN LIFE?? This was all a big mistake.

I never should've gone back to dating, because I can't handle actually liking somebody and then realizing, *Oh, but he was fucking somebody else three weeks before we met and so there's no way that he's not still thinking of her while we are in bed together! Hell, he's probably still thinking of his ex-wife of 20-plus years. This is a landmine.*

Even if he's not actually thinking of her, I can't stop thinking that he is. You think I like that feeling? I know there's nothing he can do about it except try to understand my perspective. This is all a little outside my normal range of experience.

I do not have any expectations beyond next month. I am only holding on loosely, and I am not going to tie my boat to his sails.

Why isn't he texting?? It's been two hours!

I don't want him to feel responsible for my well-being. I can handle that responsibility by now. This is territory I never expected to be in again.

I know I should just take each day as it comes and see where that leads.

Oh, yes, absolutely. That's what I'm trying to do.

One day

at a time

but I'm an obsessive planner!

Then he starts with the bitmojis from work. So then I have to as well. I tell you those stickers are the downfall of the English language. They are immature as hell; the avatars look like some 16-year-old girl. I am literally texting STICKERS! Like we used to put on our Trapper Keepers.

(Three hours later)

This is a long time with no texts.

I guess he spoiled me.

This is why texting sucks.

Have I become a text addict?

I will probably fuck things up by the end of the month anyway.

Remember I try to keep my expectations low. Very. Very. Low.

Nobody's perfect.

It's a vicious cycle.

Thinking I will fuck things up makes me fuck things up

because I get anxious about fucking things up.

If only I had the self-esteem men have.

If only I liked myself like men love themselves.

Sometimes I do.

There has been research on this.

I need to spend way more time feeling good about what I have accomplished instead of bad about what I have not accomplished.

Not going to send an X-rated bitmoji.

I have decency standards.

I'm just trying to keep up.

I know, it's tough for my liberally educated mind

or limitedly educated.

He should feel at least a little bit spoiled being with such an amazing woman.

In her beautiful home, in her beautiful brain.

So much beauty.

You want me to be modest?

How modest are you?

I'm an extremist.

Either I have a superiority complex or an inferiority complex, depending on the day.

Women are not superior to men.

We are completely and totally equal, in every way.

Well, except for the genitals and other parts.

Though, of course, "equal" does not equate to "the same."

No, who would want that?

I don't think I should wear anything too risqué or outfits that would overshadow him.

I know he hates to be upstaged.

Should I wear white?

The same outfit I wore on the first date?

Very virginal, and very bridal.

I think he likes white.

He must think I am hot!

I just want to jump up on my soapbox.

I laugh at his jokes all the time.

He said he was looking for someone who could appreciate his snarky sense of humor.

Or rather, "quirky."

Why do I feel like I'm always being roasted?

He must be a little bit crazy to want to hang out with somebody as crazy as I am.

Insane people tend to hang together; we have to.

Maybe he runs a sex trafficking ring.

Maybe he's with the Russian mafia.

Maybe he's in bed with Trump.

Maybe he's bisexual.

Maybe he's in an open marriage.

Maybe it's gonna take me a while before I really trust somebody.

There are so many horror stories about women inadvertently dating married men.

It's entirely possible he could be in an open marriage.

And everyone knows, even his parents.

Stranger things have happened.

I hate texting.

He's lucky I got over the other crazy stuff I told myself to stop thinking.

My mind can go to the darkest place imaginable. I have to reel it back in.

I need to remind myself that some things are better left unsaid, but I also need to feel like I can share my crazy thoughts with him.

How can I trust him enough to share crazy thoughts with him

AND

*Dis*trust him enough to think he is still married?

I am still trying to process that.

Women are not crazy. Guys make us this way.

It isn't just sex, it's being in the same room with a man.

Don't make me cry.

I was so happy this morning.

I woke up happy.

Really.

I have to adjust.

I can't explain it. It's like I've never done it before.

I did not think he would take it so seriously.

Because we both know it's crazy.

I'd rather be crazy with you than sane without you.

Yes, I texted that. I think that's the nicest thing I have ever said to a man.

Then again, I am crazy either way.

But what exactly does crazy entail?

It means I will speak my mind even when it could make me appear socially and/or sexually unacceptable. No. Not *appear*. I *am*, in reality, unacceptable to most people. Expressing our feelings even though someone might say we are being too sensitive or overreacting, that is what men mean when they call a woman crazy.

It's always the women who are crazy. Why?

What if I reverse it?

Sane with you, crazy without?

I am crazy *either way*.

I can't win.

Yes. I hate this texting thing.

Why do I like to have sex in the dark?

Certain senses are intensified if others are switched off.

My frontal cortex latches on to anything that snags the flow of sensations and pulls me back into the analytical sphere.

And one thing I am very critical of is my body.

With my age and background, how could I not be? Really.

There is freedom in the dark.

That must be why I am a night owl.

It doesn't have to be pitch black.

My bedroom is a dark room because I often sleep till noon. Or take naps during the day.

For example, talking during sex, regardless of the content, is often a distraction to me.

My mind will start to analyze the words used, when, why, how, and what it all really means, ad nauseum.

Then I'm not in my body anymore, I'm in my head.

And if a guy is looking at my nakedness and my "performance," I assume he is judging every square inch of me, judging my responses and actions, and then I feel like I have to put on a show. Which makes me feel like I am not "me" anymore, I'm just playing a role. And while that may work for him (because he can't tell), it means I'm not even in the room anymore. Just like the scene from *Annie Hall*, when she has an out-of-body experience during sex, and her soul leaves the bed, sits on a chair, and watches from a distance.

No woman can have an orgasm while she's faking one for the benefit of someone else.

That is my basic insecurity and general self-consciousness, which afflicts many women, as we have been bombarded with images of perfect women since we were old enough to know our gender assignment.

I am willing to engage in the project and let go of some hang-ups as best I can.

I know I am not the only woman who is a little shy about having sex under bright light.

Now, maybe on the beach. Outdoor sex is a whole other thing. I have done that before. ;)

Men have not learned a thing. Even over the age of 50, they are still incapable of dealing with women as human beings. We are judged first and often SOLELY on our appearance. Men don't care what a woman has to say until they decide how they feel about how she looks, even if she is higher status than they are. In any case, they will listen or follow her lead only grudgingly, regardless of her looks. This is not whining. *This is a factual statement of a societal problem.* But can it be changed? Is it even possible for society to intercede between a man and his basic biological response to a woman? After all, this response is not conscious. Can men be faulted for being men? Can men circumvent their reptilian brain? If not, then sexism is indeed ingrained in the brain and therefore in society. It's part of the fabric of our lives. We are all still cave men and women and it is useless for anyone to try to change this. We have to work around it. And through it. And in spite of it. Which is as good as it gets.

Women will be heard. Probably the best way to speak is as a disembodied woman. And an image-free woman, so people have no choice but to take you at your *word*. And yet I think, if people know that I am a fairly good-looking woman, they are more inclined to listen to my words. Or maybe less inclined. Can't win for losing. It all comes down to the exact nature of the listener.

We have to hit rock bottom so we can bounce back up.

Art can only come into being at rock bottom.

That is where the heavy lifting is done.

The starkness of mere existence and the fear of obscurity.

The sobbing over the distinct possibility that no one cares what you have to say.

The aggravation of dealing with people who don't know

who you are

what you have done

or what you know.

The pining to give and to love, but having no idea how.

The endless stories that need telling but they get lost in the fog of so many others.

Accomplishments?

I spent the majority of my life living in survival mode.

I had no idea what I was going to do for money.

So the fact that I've spent most of my life just scrounging for an existence is no surprise

given the choices that I made and the circumstances into which I was born.

And then the cancer came.

I was already struggling.

So I shouldn't be too hard on myself for not accomplishing great things

when I was just trying to survive most of the time.

People who live in survival mode don't normally change the world.

Me: "I have a college degree. People with college degrees should not be working in strip clubs."

Cool Male Friend: "No. They should be, because men need smarter strippers."

And what do women need?

Sound business partners.

So. If I were President…

I got nothing.

Funny how at 14, I thought I had some answers. But now...

Nothing.

Besides crazy stuff, like allocating tax dollars for:

Building entire cities designed by and for women.

Separate but equal schools for girls and boys.

Rest stops with yoga yurts.

Fitmarts where a workout is embedded in the act of grocery shopping.

High-speed solar-powered rail.

Casinos owned and operated by women. (This would fund the city and the schools.)

A lie detecting app.

Oh, and an actual wearable moral compass.

I guess that could be combined with the lie detecting app.

I don't know why I want to still look young.

Young people don't get any respect,

especially young women.

I'll never get any respect if I look young.

But I'll be ignored if I look old.

There is something about living alongside a highway.

There's something about growing up along a highway.

You can't ever escape this feeling that life is passing you by,

because life is literally passing you by.

Leaving you behind.

And you wonder about each car

the people in each car

wondering where they're going and why

and if they pass by every day

or if they only pass by

once.

And they don't realize that they are driving by anyone

because the house looks like it might not even be occupied.

They don't know I'm here.

So it feels like the world does not know I'm here.

And like everyone else, I just want people to know I'm here.

But I don't know what people I'm even talking about.

And at the end of most days, I feel like I've either been hit by a bus,

or like I've been trying to keep up with one.

First they said you got to be nice

then they said you got to be pretty

then they said you got to be sexy

then they said you got to be thin

then they said you got to be rich

then they said you gotta be married

then they said you gotta have children

then they said you still got to be thin

you still got to be sexy

you still got to be rich

Then they said you got to be popular.

And finally they said,

you still got to be nice.

Fuck them.

We are a noisy place.

America.

We fill up silence with the sound of our own voices

With the sound of other voices

With advertisements, with images, with admonishments, and numbers

With sounds of gadgets and vehicles

With the dull roar of traffic and muffled speech from the apartment next door.

We don't know what silence sounds like.

We are uncomfortable alone.

We are uncomfortable with quiet.

We don't trust the quiet ones.

We judge people we don't know.

We make generalizations with no basis.

We can't admit we don't know something.

We can always ask Google. Google knows. Google is God.

We think we live in modern times.

That is what makes us so clearly crazy and full of ourselves.

We are nothing.

We are nobody.

We run from this.

"Yes, we are Somebody!"

And we point to our work profiles, scads of friends on Facebook,

to our bank accounts and investment portfolios.

"I am! Because I say so. And my bank and my family and friends say so."

The quote is "I think, therefore I am."

Are we thinking?

Who is thinking?

What are we thinking?

We're not.

We're pathetic.

And knowing this,

accepting this,

is the beginning.

We have not yet begun.

EPILOGUE

Since this book was completed well before the present time and in light of the revulsions, revelations, and revolution of summer 2020 and Black Lives Matter, I feel the need to address the social movement that has gained momentum in the interim.

Since I am not a Person of Color, it is beyond my capacity as a white person to try to comment on the Black experience in America. Yet even though I have probably had some advantages as a white person, I have also been disadvantaged in other ways that I have pointed out in this book. My own marginalization enables me to relate to the feeling of being sidelined in society. Let's not confuse privilege with power. Only the people in power have the ability to grant privileges, and some white women only have privileges mostly because a more powerful segment of society has granted them.

I can only hope that there will be systemic change in every dimension of society so that all people are enfranchised, participatory, and treated equally at all times and in all ways. This is the only way any democracy can work. A civilization must be able to *handle* democracy, handle the truth, and handle it with care, for it is the most fragile form of government, needing near constant cultivation and vigilance. Black lives matter because they are a key part of the history of American democracy. Black history is symbolic of the struggle towards liberty and justice for all.

M. B. Clark, July 2020